# I'M DONE!

*"Take Control of Your High Conflict Divorce"*

## ANDREA LaROCHELLE, RFM

# Dedication

"That which does not kill us makes us stronger."
Friedrich Nietzsche

As hard as the lessons have been to learn, and make no mistake they were hell, I thank the high conflict person in my life for giving me the opportunity to meet incredible creatives, change makers and kickass thought leaders. My life is better for having experienced the challenges you provided me.

# Acknowledgement

Bill Eddy and his team from The High Conflict Institute have been instrumental in my personal growth and professional expertise. The universe gifted me with the opportunity to research/critique the programs Bill Eddy created for parents experiencing high conflict separations/divorces - and from that day on, my path has been forever changed for the better. Not a day goes by that I don't thank Bill for his brilliance, compassion, endless curiosity and insight into the challenges of communicating with someone who is high conflict.

Before I met Bill, I was in survival mode. Each day felt like a million hours. I was always on guard and fearful of what might be coming my way next. It sounds cliché, but Bill gave me insight into high conflict behaviors and taught me the skills I needed to thrive - not just survive.

Dr. Johal and Sonia taught me how to feel my feelings, instead of eat them. Sometimes I still devour an entire box of gummy bears, but with less frequency than before. Thanks for having my back.

Diane Shearer for knowing how to push me into creativity, rather than saying 'no' to my endless ideas. Your leadership and guidance have been instrumental in allowing me to go deeper and bigger than I ever thought possible.

My friends MM, SD and DY who have listened to me endlessly as I sort through my thoughts, feelings and challenges - never judging me, always asking the right questions to spark the mental shift I needed. Thank you.

JK for instilling the confidence I needed to make this book happen - thank you for giving me the courage to believe in myself.

Pat for helping me understand and move my anger/resentment.

The High Conflict Person in my life - You lack the insight to understand the challenges you gave me, you also lack the insight to grasp how much I've grown from the experience. I now understand that I needed you, as much as you needed me. I sincerely wish you all the best as your life unfolds.

My kids - you have made me a better human. Never let anyone tell you that you can't do something. Be relentlessly curious. And feel your damn feelings - then let them go.

Mom and Dad - you never told me what to do, instinctively recognizing that I'd just do the opposite. You let me make mistakes, knowing the lessons I learned from them would serve me well. I could not have asked for better parents - thank you!

To my partner in crime - Todd LaRochelle. Thank you for riding the high conflict train with me. Who would have thought our biggest challenge would be our greatest gift - it didn't kills us and it really did make us stronger... I love you.

# Contents

# CHAPTER 1

# Manage your Emotions "Have. Feel. Move."

Use Flexible Thinking.
Moderate Your Behaviour.

It's next to impossible to use *flexible thinking* to *moderate your behavior* if you haven't learned to *manage your emotions*. Common negative emotions are *anger, fear, anxiety, stress, worry, frustration, resentment, sorrow, sadness, desperation and hate*. When these are not managed, they can create havoc in your life.

A high conflict divorce is the perfect catalyst to create all of those negative emotions, often times, all at once. A stressed out parent isn't able to moderate their behavior when a child accidentally drops a glass of milk on the floor. A parent full of hate won't be able to use flexible thinking to understand the benefits that both parents can offer in their child's life.

Living in fear that someone may criticize or use their actions against them will reduce a parent's ability to allow their children to grow and flourish.

An anxious parent breeds an anxious home and an anxious child. Almost everyone knows the toll negative emotions take on the body, mind and spirit. Physical health starts to deteriorate – sore knees, stiff neck, repeated throat infections, and weakened immune system. Your brain feels foggy, you become forgetful, and focusing on anything for more than a few minutes is challenging.

It becomes more and more difficult to find joy in day-to-day living. You're laughing less and snapping more, and you start to avoid social gatherings. Very few people know how to manage their emotions, especially their negative ones, effectively.

I've heard people suggest: "Go for a run." "Take a brisk walk" "Have a glass of wine" "Eat a piece of chocolate" "Watch a funny movie" and my all-time favorite; "Just let it go." If any of those **easy** fixes worked, why are most of us still wandering around unable to manage our emotions effectively? When you've been triggered into anger, just letting it go doesn't work.

When you're so anxious you can't sit still, watching a funny movie isn't going to calm you. When you're trying to control everything around you because you can't control the one thing you desperately want to control, eating a piece of chocolate isn't going to magically make you feel better. When you are so lost, exhausted and bewildered at your current situation that you feel paralyzed, a glass of wine isn't going to help energize you so you can change strategies.

So what does work? What can you do to help you manage your emotions? No, you can't move to Mars and disappear; you can't relocate to New York and start over; and you can't change who you had a child with. Although waving a wand and starting over right about now sounds awfully appealing, doesn't it?

In all seriousness; you want to know how to manage your emotions so that your emotions don't manage you.

Emotions are powerful. They come, they go. Sometimes they overstay their welcome. At some point during our lifetime we learned to let our emotions become our identity.

As a child you may have heard "Oh, he's an anxious child." And, he became an anxious adult. "She's always so angry." And she became an angry adult. "He's such a depressed little guy, moping around." Oh, he became a depressed adult. Or as an adult you may have adopted some negative emotions because of certain life experiences or trauma's you've been through. "He's been angry since he lost his job." "She's been anxious since they separated" "She's been walking around with her head in the clouds since her sister passed away."

Everyone responds differently to his or her emotions, both negative and positive. For example, anger can be expressed through tears, screaming, laughing, silence or scheming. There is no right way to be angry; it's a feeling that everyone has now and then. Some of us more often than others.

Sorrow can be expressed through the very same expressions as anger; tears, screaming, laughing, silence or scheming. There is nothing wrong with having those feelings. I would argue that it's important to have all those feelings, 'have' being the key word.

Have the feeling.
Feel the feeling.
Move the feeling.
Have. Feel. Move.

Most people tend to have a feeling. Fewer people feel their feeling. And almost no one moves the feeling. **We've all been there:** That moment when you snap from a calm, sane human being to an irrational, screaming nut-head. That conversation that was going smoothly until suddenly it wasn't. You burst into tears out of frustration and can't regain composure.

Those circles you keep walking in, unable to figure out why your words only seem to make the situation worse. That paralyzing anxiety that stops you from creating or implementing any real boundaries.

That silly goofiness that takes over when you think you simply can't continue with the craziness that has become your life. We've all had that eternally optimistic friend or family member who only sees life through rose colored glasses; "Life throws us curve balls to challenge us", "To help us grow and evolve", "To teach us the tools we need to move forward." Maybe you'd buy into the rose colored glasses if you could see some kind of light at the end of the tunnel. But there is no light in sight. Just a long dark space that feels like it's slowly sucking the life out of you. You can't change who you had kids with. You can't change the condescending and manipulative tone they use towards you. You can't change the often-cruel steps taken to hurt you, regardless of who else it hurts in the processes.

So what can you do? You can take responsibility for your own feelings.

Have. Feel.
Emotions are not a choice.

I've often heard professionals talk about feelings being a choice, 'you are choosing to be angry; you can choose to be less angry'. I want to give their heads a shake. Obviously, they've never been really and truly angry. The kind of angry that makes you think your head might start spinning like the girl from the Exorcist movie. I like to call real anger Exorcist Anger. Exorcist Anger makes you feel like your blood is boiling; It stops all rational thought; It makes you feel like you will either pass out or throw things. Exorcist Anger is not a choice; it's a physical reaction to real and/or imagined circumstances. Exorcist Anger is a physical.

You can't stop the fact that your body has reacted to something/someone. Your body decides whether or not it will have Exorcist Anger. And this is where most people get stuck. Their body has a reaction to something/someone and then they have Exorcist Anger. The same example can be used for any emotion: your body decides to have anxiety, have worry, have giddiness, and have resentment. Emotions are not a choice they are a reaction. This is where feeling becomes a choice. Where you chose to be Angry, Sad, Resentful, or Anxious. Since we were young, we've been conditioned not to feel. When you fell and scraped your knee, you were told 'It's okay, get up and brush it off.' When you cried because you didn't get picked for the basketball team, you were told to 'Suck it up and stop crying.' When someone told you to 'Stop being sad because little Johnny hurt your feelings.' When you were told 'Life isn't fair, stop being angry' or your sister got the bigger piece of birthday cake, on your birthday. We're bred from a young age not to feel our feelings.

Somewhere in history feelings became something to fear, to avoid, to squash. But something has to happen to that physical response you had to something and/or someone. If you don't feel your feelings, you'll either get stuck in having them or find feeling masks. Some people eat their feelings. Others smoke their feelings. Some do drugs, create sex addictions, become hoarders or perfectionists. It's that simple. If you get stuck in having feelings and don't learn to feel your feelings, they will start to feel you. And it ain't pretty. So how, after years/decades of not feeling feelings, do you learn to actually feel? The answer is easy, but it takes a lot of practice, and planning, because when you're triggered into having a feeling, your rational thought processes go out the window.

You have to have a plan. You have to know what you are going to do the next time you are triggered into Anger, Worry, Resentment, or Sadness. If you don't have a plan, you'll get stuck in 'have' instead of moving on the Steps to move from 'have' to 'feel.'

You need to start recognizing how, when and why you get triggered into having a feeling. What happens to you physically when you get angry? Have an anxiety attack? Fall into sadness?

It's vitally important to become aware of your physical reactions to the feelings you are having. Once you know your physical reactions to having a feeling, you can learn to feel the feeling.

When you're triggered into a feeling, get down and dirty with the physical reaction your body is having. Triggered into Exorcist Anger? Feel every ounce of blood pumping through your veins; Get lost in that dizzy feeling you get because all the blood has left your brain; Excuse yourself and go somewhere safe and private to throw things, punch a heavy weight bag, pound a table with your fist.

Give yourself 5 minutes to feel every last ounce of anger, sadness, worry or resentment your body has been triggered into having. Seriously, set a timer. Feeling your emotions for 5 minutes is hard. Our head wants to take over and start thinking, planning, strategizing. But if you're thinking, you're not feeling. And if you're not feeling, you're getting stuck in having. And you've been programmed into getting stuck in having, so getting into feeling will be a challenge. Do it anyways.

from the high conflict relationship and feel like I was slowly regaining control of my high conflict situation. Six months of *working* through some tough questions. Six months of *actively seeking* out my emotional triggers. Six months of *creating* and *implementing* boundaries to protect myself. Six months of *developing* coping mechanisms for when I was emotionally triggered.

While those were a challenging six months – full of introspection, confusion, anger, anxiety and exhaustion – I can honestly say that I am now 95% emotionally disengaged from the high conflict relationship I was in. Roughly once a year, I let my guard down and forget the strategies I have put into place to ensure I stay disengaged from the conflict. But what's important is that I don't let it derail me for longer than a week. I have strategies in place that allow me to quickly regroup and refocus on my purpose for staying disengaged.

## It is vitally important to understand what your emotional triggers are before you can begin the disengagement process.

How can you disengage from something if you don't know what got you engaged in the first place? Without that base understanding, you will continue to be triggered without even knowing you are being triggered. Your #1 goal right now is to create emotional disengagement from the high conflict parent so that you are better able to manage yourself and help your children through their separation/divorce challenges.

## Who Are *High Conflict People* Disclaimer:

Bill Eddy, with the High Conflict Institute, has developed a working theory and definition of High Conflict People:

- ✓ It is not a personality disorder and it is not in the DSM.

- ✓ I am not a Doctor. I am not telling you your co-parent has a High Conflict Personality.

- ✓ You are not a Doctor. Or maybe you are, but not one who has been hired to diagnose the other parent.

- ✓ Do not attempt to diagnose the other parent with a High Conflict Personality.

- ✓ Do not tell the other parent you think they have a High Conflict Personality.

- ✓ The information provided in this document is to give you insight as to how High Conflict Personalities see the world, to help you better understand why your co-parent reacts the way they do so you can learn how best to communicate with them.

## The Importance of DISENGAGING

A magic wand can't be waved to have your emotional triggers instantly disappear, nor will Harry Potter arrive and cast a spell on your co-parent making him/her suddenly rational. High Conflict Personalities do not change. Part of what makes people a High Conflict Personality is that they have narcissistic tendencies. Narcissists believe they are always right. And they will spin every conversation, every email, and every experience they have to meet their need to be right in their heads.

## The High Conflict Personality lens is always the same; they are right and you are wrong.

Just because they believe they are right and you are wrong, just because they say it, just because they try to convince the world of it – doesn't make it true. Parents who are the non-high conflict parent often spend countless hours/days/months/years trying to figure out how to make the parenting relationship better. Surely there is a book or a course that can help you determine how to deal with someone who is so irrational? If you could just figure out how to get through to the other parent, to help them understand your point of view, to encourage them to see how the conflict is hurting the children?

## Nothing you say or do will change the other parent's behaviour.

Dr. Phil says it best: "If you always do what you've always done, you'll always get what you've always got." And you've long heard about the definition of insanity: doing the same thing over and over and expecting different results.

Was the other parent the perfect parent while you were together? No. That's one of the reasons you aren't together anymore. So why are you expecting the behavior to change now that you're apart? You know the other parent isn't going to change, ever. You can't depend on them to help change the direction of the conflict.

## You can only change how you respond to the conflict.

You can't change what you don't know. Understanding your emotional triggers allows you to figure out why you keep engaging in conflict cycle with your co-parent. If a tree falls in the forest and no one is around to see or hear it, does it still make a noise? The same is true for conflict. If you don't engage in the conflict the other parent stirs up, is there still conflict? Figuring out your triggers and having a plan for when you are triggered will help you move towards disengagement, or as I like to call it: freedom.

Once you are disengaged, or in "freedom", his/her words won't sting any more. The control he/she once had over your life will disappear. You won't expect him/her to change and won't be surprised by attacks on you personally, or as a parent. Wouldn't it be nice to have the kind of relationship with your children's other parent that other people have? You have coffee together to plan the summer schedule; you attend birthday parties, parent teacher interviews and Christmas concerts together. It's a beautiful ideal – one to strive towards for sure. But you can't get there alone.

You are separated/divorced from a High Conflict Personality. You are separated/divorced from one of the most challenging personalities there is to co-parent with. You may never have that pretty white picket fence separation/divorce. You need to let go of that expectation and live in the present. The white picket fence separation/divorce idealism is unlikely. You and your co-parent will never be friends, but you don't need to be friends.

You calmly and purposefully respond to challenges in your path of creating a successful "company."

## Your goal is to move towards a Business Professional Relationship.

Imagine you are two CEOs of a company with nothing in common but the mutual desire to build a Fortune 500 successful company; two CEOs of a company with very different views on how to build that successful company; two CEOs of a company who have to figure out how to communicate with each other to ensure that company is successful.

That successful company is *your children, a*nd one of the CEOs has a High Conflict Personality, which means he/she thinks his/her way is always right and your way is always wrong. Fighting CEOs result in a failed company. You are the only CEO who can ensure the conflict between you two remains minimal. The other CEO is a High Conflict Personality, and doesn't know he/she is a High Conflict Personality and will do his/her best to provoke you to create more drama and conflict. The other CEO doesn't understand that he/she's destroying the company. The other CEO genuinely believes his/her way is the right way to success, but you know better.

You know reduced drama and reduced conflict is the only way to grow a successful Fortune 500 company. It isn't fair that one CEO has to do all the work, but nothing in business is fair. So you do the work. You figure out your triggers. You figure out how to disengage from the drama and conflict the other CEO creates. You calmly and purposefully respond to challenges in your path of creating a successful company.

## The Need To PLEASE

Do you ever lay awake at night wondering how the heck you got into this mess in the first place? You are an intelligent, likeable human being. How did you end up with someone who has a High Conflict Personality? And what made you think having kids with them was a good idea? You aren't alone.

Virtually everyone who is not a High Conflict Personality has been there and thought that. And almost no one has figured out why they ended up in a relationship with someone who emotionally, mentally, financially and sometimes physically dragged them through the dirt. Often times they even repeat the cycle and end up with a 2nd or 3rd High Conflict Personality. The need to please is deep-rooted and was nurtured long before you met the person you had children with.

Most people would say they aren't pleasers; that they are strong and independent. How do they explain having children with someone who isn't capable of allowing someone to be strong and independent? From a very young age people learn that when you please someone, they smile. When you don't please someone, they are indifferent towards you. Voila, the need to please is created. Often, pleasers go through life trying to please others and often don't even know that is what they are trying to do. Pleasing someone creates an adrenaline high, and validation that we are **good enough**. Along the way, pleasing someone became the only way you received validation that you were good enough.

As a result you sought out people to please – parents, teachers, friends, colleagues, employers and spouses.

When you first met your High Conflict Personality former spouse, you were attracted to the energy, the flair for drama, the ability to take control of a situation, the ability to sing your praises really loudly when you pleased him/her…which only fueled your need to please. You say things like:

- ✓ Wow, this person who seems to have so much charismatic energy thinks I'm awesome.

- ✓ Wow, when I please him/her, he/she builds me up to be bigger than life.

- ✓ Wow, with him/her in my life, I am **good enough.**

**Then you move to:**

- ✓ Wow, I better not screw this up.

- ✓ Wow, it's getting harder and harder to please him/her.

4. **What emotion does the other parent hope to spark in you when he/she presses your buttons? Anger? Anxiety? Fear?** If you don't know what emotion you are feeling when your buttons are pressed, you aren't going to know which emotion you need to work through.

5. **What tone does the other parent use that you interpret as hostile?** Condescending is a common one. If your co-parent's condescending tone is pressing your buttons, you are caring too much about what they think of you.

6. **What drives your need to defend yourself against the other parent's attacks?** It's natural in nature to defend yourself when you're attacked. The purpose of defending yourself in nature is protect yourself from death. The other parent isn't going to eat you for dinner and they aren't going to stop attacking your character or your parenting, regardless of how you defend yourself.

7. **Why do your co-parent's lies cause you to get angry?** Everyone close to you knows the other parent is a liar. Your children may not know it yet (do not tell them) but one day they will be adults and reflect on their childhood, and then they will know too.

8. **What if all the other parent's criticisms of you and your ability to parent were true, what**

**would you do differently?** Think hard on this. If you wouldn't do anything differently, why are you letting their words make you feel the need to defend yourself? **Is your parenting good enough just the way it is?** Sometimes there is some truth to what the other parent says about our parenting skills and us. If you are 100% confident that your parenting is **good enough** then stop listening to the words telling you it isn't.

9. **Why do you keep expecting your co-parent to behave differently?** People don't change overnight, they are who they were while you were together. And they didn't change while you were together, so why would they change now?

10. **What would it feel like to get an email/phone call from the other parent and have them say horrible, manipulative things to you and not feel anything? No anger. No need to defend yourself. No anxiety that what they are saying might be true.** You've lived in anger/fear for a very long time, it's all you've known for as long as you can remember. You need to start feeling how it feels to not engage in conflict so you know what feeling you're working towards.

11. **What's stopping you from disengaging in the conflict you are experiencing with the other parent?** There is a reason you haven't disengaged

yet, what is it? Sometimes what we know is comfortable, so we hang out there, even though it's toxic.

12. **When are you triggered? Daily? Hourly? Weekly?** Understanding when you are triggered allows you to figure out which boundaries you need to create around the timing of your communication with the other parent. Do they text you 10 times a day? Call you with ridiculous requests? Email you novels critiquing your parenting weekly? A communication plan is key, but you need to understand your needs before you make one.

13. **What if you responded to emails every 72 hours (or once a week) instead of immediately? What's the worst that could happen? Would you be taken to court?** If you put a boundary in place that all communication will be responded to within 72 hours (and tell the other parent about the boundary and follow through on it), it's highly unlikely that a Judge would slap your wrists.

14. **Your co-parent has a High Conflict Personality, which means they gain power and momentum from drama and conflict. What would happen if you stopped reacting? Stopped fueling their need for drama and**

**conflict?** Changing the dance you're used to is scary for both of you. Planning out what to expect from the other parent, and yourself, as you begin this process will help you stay on the path of disengagement when it gets tough. Your old dance is easy, the new one is going to take some time learning the new steps.

15. **What boundaries can you put in place to protect yourself from becoming triggered?** If emails trigger you, have a friend or professional read them and tell you how to respond. If seeing him/her during child exchanges presses your buttons, create a new model for exchanges.

16. **What do you say or do that triggers the other parent?** It may seem like all you have to do is breath and they get angry but chances are if you look a little deeper, they too have triggers. Once you know what they are, you can avoid them, or press them, if you really feel like continuing to fight.

17. **Knowing only you can change the conflict cycle, that the other parent will never change, what can you do differently in your communication?** They write you novels for emails, but if you do the same, do they read them?

18. **What behaviors do you want to model for your children? How do you want them to**

**resolve conflict when they are adults?** Children learn what they live. What do you want them to learn?

19. **What would your life look like in 10 years if you changed nothing and continued communicating the same way you have been?**

# CHAPTER 3

# Decide

## "How To Make Difficult Decisions With Difficult People"

You've probably never had to make so many decisions before in your whole life. What will the parenting schedule be? What is best for the kids? Why does all the research contradict itself? How will we decide which sport or activities our kids will be registered for? Who will take the kids to the doctor or dentist? Do we attend parent teacher interviews together? Do I have to ask to get the kids haircuts? What is the best way for us to communicate so our kids don't see us fight?

Parents in low levels of conflict have the luxury of being able to figure out a lot of their answers through regular communication. But if you're reading this book, you're not experiencing low levels of conflict. You are stuck in the murky, smelly, destructive home of high conflict decision making. Every decision you try to make creates an argument, an attack on your character, your ability to parent – leaving you baffled and without an outcome or every decision is made for you. You are told how things are going to unfold for your children, leaving you with no input or say into how your children are raised or you are served a court application and affidavit each time you disagree with what your Ex tells you needs to happen. I know exactly how this feels.

> Exhausted. Guarded. Angry. Fearful.
> Anxious. Resentful.

And then one of three things happen;

1) You put off making the decision. Avoidance becomes easier than the possible reaction you may get from your Ex.

2) You stick your heels in and force the issue over something that you didn't want just because you are sick and tired of being bullied.

3) You give in to whatever the demands are. Giving in is easier than trying to negotiate, and the cycle continues.

As each day goes by, your right become more of a shell of who you used to be.

Trying to make decisions with the high conflict personality in my life was like walking on a tight rope – if I didn't say the right thing at the right time, I'd get pushed off into the safety net – except there was no safety net. I'd hit the ground hard, each and every time. If I said black, he'd say white. If I gave in and agreed to white, he'd say black. It really didn't matter what I said, I was always wrong, which is an important lesson for you to understand. When you are co-parenting with someone who may have a high conflict personality, it doesn't matter what the issue is. If one issue is resolved, another one will always surface. "The issue isn't the issue" is what Bill Eddy of the High Conflict Institute always reiterates. People with high conflict personalities do not have the skill set to manage their issues appropriately, so they just keep creating them because if there is an issue, there is drama. High Conflict Personality's (HCP's) thrive on drama. Drama is their comfort zone. While most of us freeze or panic during conflict, an HCP's heart rate slows down and they become calm. Awesome (note sarcasm). Don't worry, there is hope.

First let's figure out why HCP's love drama so much, why they have made it their comfort zone and have no intention of changing. When someone is a healthy, functioning, rational human being, their brain functions work properly. Their thought processes sway back and forth between their right and left sides of their brain. What does this mean? And how does it affect you?

Let's examine the role of each side of the brain.

The left side of the brain is responsible for being Analytical, Logical, Repetitive, Organized, Detailed, Scientific, Detached, Sequential, Rational Thought and Reasoning.

The positives of people using the left side of their brain is that they are able to be rational, have insight into their own behavior, understand consequences and have a reasonable conversation.

The negatives of people who get stuck in their hand brain is that they lack creative problem solving skills, aren't overly empathetic and often appear detached from the outcome.

The right side of the brain is responsible for Being Creative, Imaginative, General, Intuitive, Conceptual, Big picture, Negative emotions and Irrational thought

The positives of people who are right brain dominant; they are creative and imaginative problem solvers, empathetic towards others, insight into their own actions and the actions of others.

The negatives of people who get stuck in their right brain; they get caught in negative emotions (conflict), aren't able to have insight into their own behavior and lack the ability to have a rational conversation. Everyone has a dominant side, left or right, but most people can transition into their non-dominant side relatively easily.

Right brain dominant people are generally Artists, Beauticians, Politicians, Athletes, Craftsman, and Actors.

Left-brain dominant people are generally Scientist, Lawyer, Engineer, Accountant and Computer Programmer.

There is a small piece of brain matter that separates the left and right brains; it's called the corpus callosum. It is believed that the corpus callosum acts as the channel in which brain messages are sent back and forth – from the left side to the right side and back again.

So, when someone is a healthy, functioning, rational human being, it is believed that their brain functions are working properly because their corpus callosum is optimal size for messages to be sent back and forth.

When someone struggles with managing their emotions, their behavior and their thinking – like someone who may be a High Conflict Personality – it is believed that the corpus callosum is the root cause. Research is suggesting that when the corpus callosum is not large enough for messages to go back and forth freely, people get stuck in one side of the brain or the other.

If you are co-parenting with someone who may be a high conflict personality, the likely cause is their corpus callosum is a little too small and they have gotten stuck in the right side of their brain (inflexible thinking, no insight, unmanaged emotions – conflict and drama).

How do you get these people back into the land of the rational? You force them there.

It's not easy. They will rebel.

They will push and scream and throw a tantrum. Ignore the drama (which is what they are trying to distract you with) and stick to your guns.

Revisit Disengage if you need tips and strategies to ignore the drama. Forcing HCP's out of the drama infused right side of their brain and into their left problem solving side of their brain will allow you to better manage making decisions with them.

You've probably noticed that when you try to communicate with your high conflict Ex that they end up talking in circles, mostly condescending put downs about you and your parenting skills, but rarely is a decision reached or maybe your Ex just tells you the outcome before a conversation is even had?

I find HCP's like to talk for the sake of hearing themselves talk. They don't usually have anything important to say, but they talk as if they do. The more they talk, the more drama they can create, and we know how frustrating it is to enter into a conversation that we've been anxious about having, only to leave feeling even more confused, lost and bewildered. So how do you change that? How do you enter into a conversation – email or in person – and shift your right brain thinking into their left-brain so you can get something accomplished.

I've created a 2-step Decision Making Process for you to keep it easy:

## 1. Have An Agenda

Seems so simple, yet so many people forget to make one. Parents enter into conversations with a loosey goosey idea of what they want to talk about, what decisions they need to make. They are so anxious about having the conversation that once they enter into it, they forget what it is they were wanting to talk about.

If you and your Ex are experiencing high levels of conflict, you need to make sure you're prepared. If you aren't, then you haven't fully prepared yourself for the conversation and you're more likely to get off track, talk too much about topics that don't matter and end up triggered. Being triggered = Being in an Emotion. If you are in an emotion and talking to your high conflict personality ex, nothing good can come of it. So make an agenda. Talk only about what is on the agenda. Your HCP Ex will try and steer you off course – so plan for it, look at your agenda to bring you back to the topics you need to talk about.

Your HCP Ex want an emotional experience, they want drama. They have no interest in making any decisions with you. They want to criticize you, belittle your efforts, minimize your parenting and shatter your confidence. You will have to use your skills to stay strong, remain disengaged and focused on the end result.

## 2. Make Proposals

The next time you are having a conversation with someone who is venting, notice what they are doing. They are usually stuck in an emotion, not making plans to change anything and talking about the past. They are stuck in the right side of their brain. Think about some of your most recent conversations or email exchanges with your Ex. Were they right brain emotional circle talking about the past or were they left-brain future action focused?

For some reason, our brain likes to hang out in the past. But that doesn't mean we can't train them to think about the future. It just takes a little work.

Bill Eddy, with the High Conflict Institute, says that any problem from the past can be turned into a proposal about the future. You just need to know how. Change the focus of the conversation from talking about the past to problem solving the future.

By making a proposal, you are solving a past problem while proposing a solution for the future. Let me give you an example.

Proposal: "I propose we divide the Easter holidays equally, allowing our children to spend time with both of us."

That proposal sounds a lot better than: "You're so selfish, you never let me see the kids during special occasions and our separation agreement says I'm entitled to half of all holidays."

See the difference?

The proposal solves a past problem (not having equal time with the kids during special occasions) and creates a plan for the future. No blame, no defensiveness, no emotionally charged put downs. Now, that's not to say that your co-parent isn't going to lash out at you and try to get you into an attack/defend yelling match – but if you have put the work into an agenda and your proposal, so you know why it is you are entering into the conversation/email exchange in the first place, you'll better be able to disengage from the invitation to fight and focus on redirecting the conversation to the topic at hand.

## How To Make Proposals

Who does…What… When and…Where

Notice that Why is not a part of the Proposal Process. Think about the word 'why' and why you use it, and how you feel when you hear it? Why can be a tricky word, often putting people on the defensive, depending on the tone of voice that accompanies it. If you're in conflict and wanting to get some decisions made, we want to reduce any possible trigger we can to ensure success.

When someone hears why, they hear judgment, even if judgment wasn't the intent. Proposals are not about the why, they are about the action. Try not to focus on why you are asking (or why your co-parent is asking) and focus on making a decision regardless of why the question is being asked. Most problems have more than one solution... but those solutions never get the opportunity to be explored because a fight usually erupts prior the exploration.

How can you manage your co-parent when they say no to your proposal? Ask them to make a counter proposal. They aren't going to want to, they are going to want to hang out in their emotional right brain. They are going to want to know why you made the proposal, what your 'motives' are. They are going to want to put you down, criticize your parenting and whatever else they say when they are trying to poke your buttons. Don't react. Just reiterate your question, "What do you propose?" They will keep trying to push your buttons – the right brain is a cozy place to hang out.

## Do Not React

If you give in to temptation and react to their attacks, its game over to try and have a proposal based conversation to get your decisions made. Stop and try again another day. If you can manage your disengagement, stay on track and remain focused on "What's your proposal?" Your co-parent's brain will slowly shift to the left and you may get a proposal out of them - or you may not.

Learning a new dance is difficult. You may need to try more than once. It may take you 100 attempts before your co-parent starts learning your new dance steps.

## Do Not Give Up

Their brain is different than yours, it takes them a lot longer to move from the negative emotional side to the logical left side. Their corpus callosum isn't as big as yours, they will be slower to catch on. But they will catch on. "You can teach an old dog new tricks." It just takes a really long time.

So what do I do if my Ex refuses to move into his left brain and never offers up a proposal? How do decisions get made?

Try this, "I have proposed x,y and z to resolve a, b and c. Please provide your 3 proposals regarding a, b and c by Friday, otherwise I'll need to move forward with one of my proposals."

No digs, no emotions, no manipulations – but it is action focused. You have decisions to make, no point in stretching them out into a heated debate. You clearly want to work with your co-parent but if they aren't willing to work with you, decisions still need to get made.

What if your co-parent makes a proposal and you are open to it, but you just have a few questions first? Ask them, just make sure you have carefully thought them through. If you use the word why, a conflict will erupt.

Here are some possible non-threatening, left brain focused, questions to ask: "What would your proposal look like in action?" "What is your picture of how this would work for you? For me? For our kids?"

Your answers to when, what, where and how will get answered with the above questions, without the other parent feeling judged or defensive.

Let's try to put it into action.

## Proposals Practice # 1:

John and Lori have a 5 year old son, Ernie. They have separated and not speaking amicably with each other. They both love Ernie and want what is best for him. They need to decide how to communicate with each other about decisions regarding Ernie as he grows up.

For each of the following questions; write a proposal. Remember, there are no wrong proposals.

    1) How do you propose John and Lori should communicate with each other (email, phone, text, in person)?

Routinely:                   Emergencies:

> 2)  What are 2 types of decisions that John and Lori will need to make jointly for Ernie's best interests?

> 3)  What are 3 types of decisions John and Lori can make on their own about Ernie, without consulting with the other parent?

> 4)  As a 5 year old, what are two types of decisions Ernie could make on his own?

Write a proposal for John that you think they might both agree to.

## Proposals Practice # 2:

John and Lori would like to develop a shared parenting plan. John has read that 50/50 is best for kids, Lori has read that until the age of 6, kids do better with a primary residence with generous involvement from the other parent.

Their mediator has told them both that the best plan for children is one that their parents can agree on.

### Lori's First Proposal

"I read an article that says it is best for young children to have one primary household but that the other parent should be involved every week. I propose that Ernie reside with me most of the time but that he spends generous amounts of time with you as well. I propose you would have 1 day and 1 overnight with Ernie, as well has half of all major holidays or we can alternate."

**John responds,** "What day and overnight were you picturing that I have each week?"

"I was thinking you'd have Friday night and all day Saturday's each week."

"I would say no to that as I read an article that says it's best for children to have roughly equal time with each parent. Instead, I propose that Ernie spend 6 days and nights with me in a two week period, so you would have 8 days and nights in a row during the same time period. I recognize that he has spent most of his time with you up until now. Once he's six, I'd like a 50-50 schedule."

"Which nights were you thinking of having with him?"

"I'd like a weekday overnight every week, like Wednesday's and I would like alternate weekends Friday at 5pm through Monday morning at school one weekend and just a Friday overnight the following weekend."

"My answer is No. I think Ernie is too young to be spending that much time away from me, as I've been the primary caregiver all of his life. And it seems like a lot of back and forth for him, transitions are hard on kids. Having said that, I am open to consider more time than I had originally proposed, especially as he gets older."

"But I want to be fully involved in his growing up — weekdays with his schoolwork as well as weekends…"

## John's Second Proposal

Usually when we hear the word no, we get defensive and angry. And when we get defensive and angry, we lash out and talk about the past. "You never blah blah blah…You always blah blah blah…" Notice that when you are working with proposals, you don't need to get defensive. 'No' doesn't equate to 'you are an awful parent and I'm saying no to spite you'. 'No' simply means that you need to keep brainstorming new proposals.

When we take the drama out of our decision-making, the decisions become easier to make.

# CHAPTER 4

# Deliver

You've received an email that triggered you but you took the necessary time to move your feelings around the attacks and manipulations that were fired your way. It's been at least 24 hours since the email hit your inbox. And you feel confident that you've disengaged. You've decided that a response is required and/or you want to initiate a conversation about specific child related topic. Now what? I've got good news for you, once you've mastered Disengage and Decide – Deliver is the easy part. If, after you've read through everything below and you still don't know how to Deliver the message you want heard, then go back and reread Disengage and Decide.

When you're trying to deliver a message to someone who is high conflict, take everything you have ever learned about communication and turn it upside down. Traditional communication courses encourage you to use the word "I", to describe how you are feeling, "I feel...." But as you'll learn below, using the word "I" is the last thing you want to do when the person you are communicating with has high conflict tendencies. Your goal for delivering your message is not to write everything you want to say to your co-parent.

Your goal for delivering your message is not to defend yourself against attacks and manipulations. Your goal is to have important child related details heard by your co-parent. If you want to vent about something or defend yourself from attacks, hire a professional.

Do not vent to your co-parent.
Do not defend yourself against their attacks.

Defending yourself will only give your co-parent further ammunition to criticize, attack and manipulate you further. Nothing you say to defend yourself against the attacks will change your co-parents perception of you. Save yourself time and energy and block them out rather than reacting to them. Traditional methods of communication, when you have two semi-rational people trying to have a conversation and make decisions, simply won't work when one parent has high conflict tendencies. So stop using traditional methods.

Stop using the popular TED method for communicating with your high conflict Ex. The TED method works wonderfully if both parents are rational, but if you're reading this book – you are likely co-parenting with someone who has proven to be irrational. So what is the TED Method? How should two rational parents communicate?

## Traditional TED Method For Communication

Tell the person how you feel
Explain why you feel that way
Describe what you would like done differently

For example, I feel angry when you don't show up on time to pick John up for your parenting time. It is disrespectful towards me by not valuing my time and hurting John's feelings when you are late. I would like for you to be on time to show me that you respect me and to ensure John knows his mom/dad is making him a priority.

Tell: I feel angry when you don't show up on time to pick John up for your parenting time.

Explain: It is disrespectful towards me by not valuing my time and hurting John's feelings when you are late.

Describe: I would like for you to be on time to show me that you respect me and to ensure John knows his mom/dad is making him a priority.

Have you used a similar strategy when communicating with your Ex? How did it work for you? Notice the word 'feel' at the beginning of the first sentence - and then the feeling words used in the rest of the paragraph. The TED method will get you nowhere fast, if your co-parent has high conflict tendencies. Your Ex doesn't care how you feel and the more you tell them why you feel the way you feel, the more:

a) Disconnected they will get from what you are requesting.

b) The more they will use your feelings against you in the future.

Traditional TED method communication is like giving candy to a person who has high conflict tendencies.

It is important to remember that High Conflict Personalities do not have control over their behavior. They have no insight. They do not have the ability to self-reflect. They instinctively blame others for everything that goes wrong. They are not trying to hurt you on purpose, they just don't know any other way of communicating. They will not change. To successfully co-parent with someone who is high conflict, you must change your behavior. Your Ex may still send attacks and manipulations your way, but if you are disengaged from them – the words and lies won't be able to hurt you. The words and lies will just roll off your back.

People with high conflict tendencies are like children during the 'terrible twos' – they tantrum to try and get what they want. And similarly to a child, if you give in to the tantrum and react, they'll know that their tantrums work to get what they want and will continue to tantrum... each tantrum kicking up a notch to try and really get your attention.

The attacks and manipulations are tantrums. The next time you receive a horrible email, think of a two year old having a tantrum and do not react.

The traditional TED method of communication doesn't work – so what does?

How do you communicate with a High Conflict Co-parent?

Here are five email communication strategies to improve communication with your High Conflict Co-Parent:

# 1) Stop Attack/Defend Communication.

You can't stop the attacks from being said, but you can stop defending yourself. You know how it goes: an email pops into your Inbox, you read it, and your blood boils. The email is riddled with negative parenting comments and accusations. You instantly feel the need to defend yourself against the horrible words directed at you.

You want to somehow prove to the other parent that they are wrong. However, instead of just defending yourself, you throw in a few snide insults as well. Those comments are received as 'attacks' by the other parent. That parent reacts by defending themselves, and then throwing in a few more rude remarks while they are at it. Just like that, the Attack/Defend cycle continues.

Many parents get stuck on this merry-go-round for years and sometimes lifetimes. They are attached to what the other parent thinks or believes to be true about them. They believe that by defending themselves, they will be able to convince the other parent that they were wrong to make the attacks in the first place. How do you stop the merry go round of attack/defend communication? Disengage so you can Decide whether or not you even want to respond.

Stopping attack/defend communication will be the single most important thing you will do to regain your sanity during this challenging time.

## 2) Your email should only be 4 sentences long (or less).

You have so much to say. So many rationales for the reason you are emailing. You need to defend yourself, point out the real truth, and then propose some options for moving forward. Only you don't. Your Ex may be a High Conflict Person. The more you write, the more ammunition you're likely to give them to twist and manipulate your words into meaning something entirely different than you were intending.

You are receiving long winded emails outlining every nonexistent shady personality trait you have; you are being called names that would make almost anyone blush. Your parenting skills are being criticized and ridiculed; lies are being written about your character, values, and family. And every ounce of your being is going to want to defend yourself, correct the lies, point out the inaccuracies in the email that was sent to you.

And I'm pretty sure that's the approach you've taken up until this point.

How has it worked for you? Are you getting the results you are hoping for? Are your emails allowing the message you want to send, to be heard? Has anything changed? Has the conflict between you and your co-parent been reduced? No. Because defending yourself, your family and your values doesn't work.

Outlining the truth for your co-parent to read doesn't work.

Rationalizing with an irrational person doesn't work.

So stop doing it.

The goal for communicating with your high conflict co-parent is not to change their opinion of you – you can talk, email and text until you are blue in the face and their opinion of you will never change.

You need to change your goal. The reason you are communicating with your high conflict co-parent is to have important child related information received by them.

High Conflict People crave drama and the longer the email, the more likely it will contain an emotional word that they can attach to, rather than absorbing the information you need them to read. Keep your email communication with your High Conflict Ex to a maximum of four sentences. It's a lot easier said than done. But by only writing four sentences, it forces you to be clear and concise about the topic you are communicating about.

It's been proven that people don't like to read long paragraphs. When there are too many words on a page, people skim read rather than read for comprehension. The longer the email, the less likely it's going to be read.

## 3) Your email will not have any emotional words in it.

Emotional words are tricky – they sneak in when you least expect it. When we're communicating about our children, we're usually feeling an emotion of some sort – fear, anger, excitement... disappointment, challenges, frustration. Or maybe you're not feeling emotional about your children; maybe you're anxious or stressed about what kind of response you're going to get to the email you are sending – so you say more than you should (in person it's called nervous chatter, in email it's called writer's diarrhea).

Every single time you put an emotional word into an email, your High Conflict Ex is going to attach him or herself to that word and respond only to that word, which is what you don't want. You want to ensure your message is received the way you intended it – not twisted and manipulated into something completely different. Your Ex may still manipulate your emotionless email to mean something than what you intended – but if you remove the emotion from your email, the likelihood of that happening decreases exponentially. Emotional words include, but are not limited to, fear, worry, concern, anxious, scared, unsure, happy, excited, angry, upset, saddened, frustrated and stressed.

If you use any of the above words (or similar type words) your High Conflict Ex will respond to the word, and not the content of your email. Communicating with fact gives the perception of merit, truth and credibility. Communicating in emotion gives the perception of weakness, irrational behavior, and mixed up perceptions. There is nothing a Judge hates more than two parents who don't get along, and have emotion filled email exchanges with each other – each parent trying to out **dig** the other parent.

When you are reading books or newspaper articles – when you read about people being emotional or having an emotional response, they suddenly hold less clout in your mind. "He's stupid!" "She's an idiot." If you hear/read those words, you aren't thinking someone intelligent wrote them. You're thinking someone emotional did. As emotion goes up, the ability to be rational goes down. You are the rational parent, make sure you present that way. If, for whatever reason, a Judge ends up reading your email exchanges, you don't want the first impression to be "this person can't control their emotions, these emails are emotion based insults, clearly the person writing them isn't very rational." No, you want a Judge to read your short, emotionless, fact based emails –

giving your communication with your Ex the perception of credibility.

## 4) Your email will not contain the word "I"

This will seem petty and ridiculous, so be prepared.

If you use the word "I" in your emails, your message will not be heard.

Your High Conflict Ex will read the word "I" and immediately shut down anything that comes after it.

Your ex doesn't care about what you want, what you think, why you want what you want. And when your ex reads the word "I" – they immediately jump to "no" in their heads.

Example's using "I": "I was thinking the kids could play soccer this Spring. Both kids loved indoor soccer over the winter and it provides them with great exercise." "I feel Billy should read for 30 minutes a day to improve his reading skills." "I would really like to take the kids to Banff, Alberta to experience the mountains during Spring Break." "I am going to host Sally's birthday party at the Zoo this year." Notice the theme of the above emails – they are all child focused (which you want), but also have the word "I" in them. And if you are co-parenting with a High Conflict

Person, as soon as you use the word "I" – you've lost them.

They will twist and manipulate your words and request and turn even a simple sentence into a giant fight.

Instead, try using your child's name at the beginning of your sentence. Using your child's name will catch your co-parents attention right off the get go – increasing the likelihood that your message will be heard the way you intended it to be.

Example's using your child's name instead of "I":

"John and Sally have expressed an interest in continuing to play soccer this spring – thoughts?" "Billy's teacher has suggested we read with him for 30 minutes before bed to help him improve his reading comprehension."

"John and Sally have expressed an interest in spending some time in the mountains. For spring break we will be going to Banff, Alberta for a few days so they can experience the mountains." "Sally would like to celebrate her birthday at the Zoo this year. What dates work for you?"

See the difference? In both examples the emphasis is on the child – but when putting the child's name at the beginning of the sentence, suddenly the email becomes only about the child and not about what you want for the child.

Your goal is to have your message heard. And by putting the child's name at the beginning of the sentence, you are more likely to have success with having your message heard.

## 5) Your email will topic specific.

In an attempt to be efficient, you likely squeeze all your topics to be discussed with your co-parent into one email.

- ✓ the dental appointment
- ✓ home work that is late
- ✓ what spring activity the kids will play
- ✓ Easter break
- ✓ Could he/she please refrain from criticizing your Aunt Sheila, it's affecting the kids.

The problem with trying to be efficient is that it makes it more difficult for your message to be heard. If one of the above topics is a trigger for your co-parent, the whole response will turn into a manipulative, angry, controlling mess. A response to the above topics could be as simple as; "Kids want to play soccer, what do you think?"

## Becomes

*"I never criticize your aunt Sheila, who do you think you are telling me what to do? The kids aren't playing any sports this spring unless you want to pay for them!"*

Put the topic in the subject line of the email. Then write four sentences or less on that specific topic, with no emotional words added in. Your co-parent may respond to all your emails in one singular email, and the emails may be filled with tone and lies. You can't control the other parent and how they react/respond – you can only control yourself. But you've disengaged from their tone and their lies, you know they get stuck in their right brain – so you won't take their tone and lies personally. For example, on the subject of spring sports,

*"Sign up for spring sports is quickly approaching. Soccer versus baseball versus lacrosse versus swimming lessons. Or we can talk to Jeremy and ask him what he would be interested in playing? Please let me know by April 1st. Thanks."*

Example:

Subject: Moving

With property values dropping, I will be putting my house up for sale in June. I am looking at 3 different neighborhoods (x, y and z) as possible options for my relocation. Once I have settled on a place, I will let you know the new address. I have no intentions of requesting Johnny change schools, he is happy where he is and I will arrange transportation for him to get to and from school while he is with me.

Sincerely,

Another Example:

Subject: Income Tax exchange

Our court Order stipulates we should exchange our income tax information in May of each year to determine the child support base and section 7 numbers. I will have my income tax information ready for you on May 1st, 2xxx. Please let me know by April 15th, 2xxx when I will be receiving your information.

## 6) Your email should have a respond by date

Notice the above examples. They all have a 'respond by date'. Why is this? You are co-parenting with someone who may or may not have an undiagnosed personality disorder, someone who manipulates and controls, someone who wouldn't think twice about lying to the courts. You are changing the way you communicate with your Ex for two reasons:

1) To save your sanity (See Disengage and Decide)

2) So you can act, move forward, go to court if need be – knowing that you've covered all your bases.

There is nothing more frustrating than sending an email that requires a response, only to have it ignored. You never get a response. You never get an answer to your question. You're just left in limbo. You put a respond by date so that you can act if no response is given.

"Act" does not mean you will automatically go to court if you don't have a response by a certain date. "Act" means that if you don't have a response by a certain date, you are moving forward with what you've proposed in the email. If your Ex is disgruntled and takes you to court – you have your bases covered. You tried to communicate with your Ex, you tried to include them in the decision making process, you tried to get their input. You were clear and emotionless in your email communication regarding your request, you asked for a response by a certain date, you didn't get one. So you moved forward.

A Judge hearing the matter would (in all likelihood) review the matter and question your Ex as to why they chose court as a means of resolving the matter rather than just responding to the email. Your high conflict Ex uses avoidance as a means to control –

take back control and put in a response by date in all of your email communications. Of course, you need to be reasonable in your request. Don't put a 'respond by date' that is an hour after you send the email – that's not fair. A 'respond by date' 48-72 hours into the future is a reasonable time frame request.

# CHAPTER 5

# You Want Me To What?

# Setting Boundaries

Boundary setting is easy in concept, but hard in practice. We've all done it, made a conscious plan to respond differently next time. And when next time arrives, we're emotionally triggered into anger, fear, anxiety, frustration, confusion and being overwhelmed that we forget our conscious plan (boundary) and do exactly what we didn't want to do, react rather than respond.

Boundary setting is not a simple task, coupled with the possibility that you're in an emotionally charged high conflict separation/divorce, and it's almost harder than pulling teeth. Yet, if you want to get your sanity back, it's a necessity. If you don't create and maintain your boundaries in a high conflict separation/divorce, you risk the conflict in your life escalating even more.

I get it, you try to be empathetic and respectful in your communication with the other parent because you genuinely want to get along for the sake of your children, so you want to make the situation amicable. But when you try to be rational with someone who isn't rational (and when someone is angry, they aren't in a rational state of mind) it puts you in a position to be emotionally triggered, which makes maintaining your boundary almost impossible.

Creating boundaries will not change the other parents actions, or the language they use or outbursts. It will allow you to disengage from the conflict, providing you with the clarity you need to respond, rather than react.

## Boundary Setting

Creating boundaries is not aggressive. The goal is not to hurt the other person, or to threaten the person unnecessarily. Boundary setting is not passive. You need to be assertive with the boundaries you create.

Sometimes your boundaries don't need to be verbalized. A simple consistent shift in behavior is sufficient, so be brief and matter of fact when setting boundaries.

# CHAPTER 6

# Choosing To Disengage

Existing within a High Conflict Separation or Divorce can be the most isolating and crazy making experience a person can have. Constantly being told everything is your fault, always being criticized for your lack of parenting skills, a barrage of emails and texts filling your inbox with manipulations and lies decorated to look like an important topic relating to your children, always being on guard waiting for the next shoe to drop, when the next court application will be filed.

Disengaging from the ongoing parental conflict is challenging, never having the opportunity to ground yourself so you can work on disengaging.

Disengaging means taking the time to understand your emotional triggers, creating and implementing boundaries to protect yourself from your triggers, and learning a new approach to communicating with your child's other parent.

You cannot change the other parent's behaviour (as much as you'd like to), you can however, choose to change your own.

Disengage yourself from a conflictual communication relationship with your child's other parent to a 'Business Casual' one. It's not easy, but it will save your sanity.

## CHAPTER 7

# Christmas In Two Homes

Do you feel like your children are missing out by not spending time with both their parents on Christmas Day? Have your children become a pawn in your ongoing parental conflict and Christmas is just another example of that?

When you are falling in love, planning your future and creating a family, rarely do you envision a plan for what might happen should the relationship fail. When you first had children, you mentally created a picture of what Christmas was going to look like for your family. That picture likely didn't include sharing the holidays, alternating Christmas and New Year's, not seeing your children open presents on December 25, in essence, having Christmas in two homes.

It wasn't the picture your children mentally created for Christmas either.

Often parents focus on what their children are missing out on, rather than what they are feeling and needing. Parents worry about what they believe their children deserve, rather than what their children need. The only thing children need at Christmas (and every day for that matter) is to know that they are loved unconditionally, regardless of their parents' inability to get along.

You can't change your reality, or your children's reality, unless, of course, you and your children's other parent are able to put your differences aside and celebrate Christmas together. You need to let go of your Christmas expectations from the past and start creating new Christmas traditions. Help your children create new magical Christmas memories that they will look back on fondly.

Christmas isn't just a day celebrated on December 25th, Christmas is about the feelings and emotions we attach to the day. Those feelings and emotions can be created on any day of the year. Choose to let go of your attachment to December 25th, the day, and start creating the Christmas feelings and emotions you want your children to associate with the experience of Christmas.

## How the Heck Do You Do That?

Focus on what is important to your children, and why. Your children may ask for the newest and shiniest toy on the shelf at Toys R' Us, but if you quiet yourself and really tune into their NEEDS, you may surprise yourself to learn what they really want. Generally, as long as their mom or dad is happy on the day Christmas is celebrated, then they are happy. Your happiness is what your children need and want for Christmas this year. Choose to put on a happy face and be present with your children this Christmas, on whatever day that might be, and however Christmas might look this year.

Focus on the memories you want your children to remember when reflecting on their childhood Christmas experiences with you. Your children are going to remember Christmas one of two ways - positively or negatively. You, and only you, can help shape the memories they will have around Christmas with you. Their other parent may take them to Disneyland, buy expensive presents or, for one reason or another, put limits on how much time you are able to spend with your children at Christmas. You can't change any of that. Those are memories, good or bad, their other parent is choosing to give your children. What memories can you help create? What feelings do you want your children to connect to their Christmas experience with you?

*"I've learned that people will forget what you said, people will forget what you did, but people will never forget how you made them feel."*

*-- Maya Angelou*

Focus your time and energy on your children this Christmas. Parents often romanticize what Christmas is like for intact families; family board games by the fire, sledding and skating with hot chocolate afterwards, caroling while decorating the Christmas tree, laughs of joy Christmas morning. Intact families have their Christmas struggles too. They argue over who knotted the Christmas lights, who will take little Joey to the walk in clinic because he sprained his ankle sledding or skating. Intact families bicker through Christmas Day because the kids were up at 5am to see what Santa brought and fifteen people are showing up for dinner.

There is a difference between intact families and those who are apart. Children of intact families celebrate one Christmas with Santa, one Christmas dinner, and one Christmas tree decorating adventure. Children of separated parents have the opportunity to experience not only two Christmas's with Santa, two Christmas dinners and two Christmas tree decorating adventures; children of separated parents also experience one-on-one Christmas time with each parent.

Cherish the time you have with your children this Christmas, whether it's on December 25th or January 8th. Make Christmas special for your children. Focus your time and energy on your children this Christmas; I promise you, they will always look back fondly on their Christmas experiences with you.

Here are five new Christmas traditions for children with two homes:

1) Celebrate half Christmas on June 25th - who decided Christmas had to be celebrated in December, anyways?

2) The great annual Christmas Pancake cook-off - create memories through feelings and emotions, this can happen any day of the year!

3) The Annual Scrabble/Monopoly/Board Game Challenge (8 hours of continuous board games - think of the laughs to be had)

4) The Annual Dollar Store Scavenger Hunt - Each family member gets $5 and 5 minutes to find the perfect holiday gag gift for everyone in their family or each family member gets $5 and 5 minutes to find the perfect gift to donate to a family in need. You can spin this many ways; What's important is that you are doing it together, creating positive emotional memories for your children.

5) The Christmas Card Craft Extravaganza - Spend a morning making Christmas Cards for your neighbours, then deliver!

# CHAPTER 8

# But It's Not Fair!

I hear the statement "But it's not fair" daily from clients, often several times an hour. "It's not fair that I only see the kids 50% of the time." "It's not fair that the kids can't see me on my birthday." "It's not fair that he/she gave up on the marriage and I'm the one suffering." "It's not fair that I can't see or speak with my kid's every day." "It's not fair that he/she was an absent parent while we were together and now she/he are super mom/dad." "It's not fair that I have to pay child support."

Merriam-Webster Dictionary defines fair as, "agreeing with what is thought to be right or acceptable: treating people in a way that does not favor some over others: not too harsh or critical."

Well that sounds reasonable. The definition of fair essentially means to have a reasonably kind and mutually respectful relationship with your child's other parent for the sake of your children. Yet so many parents are saying what they are experiencing with their child's other parent isn't fair.

Like beauty, fair is in the eyes of the beholder. If you wanted something in your divorce and got it, chances are you would view the outcome as fair. If you wanted something in your divorce and didn't get it, you'd view the outcome as unfair. What parents often forget is that divorce isn't fair. Rarely is the decision to end a relationship mutual. Rarely do both parents feel only one parent should have all the decision making authority and time with the children. Rarely (never) do either parents in divorce end up financially ahead.

What the Merriam-Webster Dictionary's definition left out is that fair is a perception created by parents to meet their own needs and wants. And unless your needs and wants are met during the separation & divorce process, you'll feel the process/ agreement/outcome is not fair. How do you shift your perception of fair? How do you get to a place with your child's other parent where you feel the process/agreement/outcome is fair?

# 1) Look at the perception of fair through your child's eyes.

What does fair look like to him/her? This is where it can get tricky; Oftentimes parents claim their needs and wants are what's best for their child. Their parental needs and wants 'agenda' ends up trumping the child's needs and wants.

Fair to your child would be having intact parents, not separated ones. Fair to your child would be having parents who got along; Parents who listened to his/her needs rather than positioning themselves to be the better parent; Parents who didn't create a tug-of-war with the child being the rope; Parents who accepted that divorce and separation isn't fair, and rather than dwelling on it, made the best of it. Create a perception of fair in your child's eyes. While his/her parents may not be together, at least they aren't fighting.

# 2) Challenge your individual perception of fair.

I often hear parents who are in the midst of creating a parenting plan that they just want it to be fair, but when pressed to define what fair looks like, they aren't able to. "I think it's fair that I have the kids full time." "I think it's fair that I make all the decisions for the children." "I think it's fair he/she only sees the kids twice a month." "I think it's fair that kids always spend Christmas with me." "I think it's fair that I plan all the kids' birthdays." "I think it's fair that I spend the child support on XYZ. I deserve a little pleasure after all the work I put into raising the kids."

When you find yourself saying these statements, what you're really saying is, "I didn't end the relationship. I think it's fair that I get everything I want. He/she has to pay for the decisions they made." "He/she was an absent parent when we were together, how dare he/she think they can now get more time with the kids now." "I hate my child's other parent more than I love my child"

When you chose to fight with your child's other parent over what you perceive to be fair, you are engaging in a conflict with someone you are choosing to hate more than you love your child. If you were genuinely putting your love for your child first, you would not be getting stuck on your perception of what's fair with your child's other parent.

## 3) Question your child's other parent's perception of fair.

If you are struggling to figure out why your child's other parent is so stuck on a certain topic or decision, question them on why they feel their position is so strong. And I don't mean, "Why on earth do you think the kids should be with you 50% of the time?" – that will just get you an argument.

If you really want to understand where your child's other parent is coming from on a certain topic or decision, it is imperative that you ask your questions without a tone and with genuine curiosity.

You may not always like the answer, sometimes you'll have to reframe your questions to dig deeper, but if you ask the right questions, you'll gain a better understanding of your co-parents perception of fair. For example, "Help me understand why it's important to you that our children live with each of us 50% of the time." 99% of the time, the other parent will answer with, "Because it's fair."

With genuine curiosity (not shock and disgust) ask a follow up question to dig deeper, "I understand that 50/50 is perceived to be fair for both of us, equal time with the children. That's not what I'm asking. I want to know why it's important to you."

Parents often struggle to put words to 'why' they want what they want. A parent could say they want 50/50 parenting for a variety of fair perceived reasons, that when gently pushed for clarity, don't really equate to 50/50 parenting.

When you are working towards creating a parenting plan and you either hear yourself using the word fair, or hear it out of the other parents mouth; You know it's time to start digging a little deeper to figure out the perception you, or the other parent, has attached to concept of fair.

# CHAPTER 9

# Three Communication Patterns Of High Conflict Parents

You have just written the perfect email to your children's other parent. You have used all the tools in your tool box to ensure your email is Brief, Informative, Friendly and Firm. You've had three people read the email over to make sure you haven't missed any added emotion or dig.

You cross your fingers and toes that this time, the issue at hand (insert issue creating conflict; Can Susie play hockey this season? Can Bobby get a haircut? How will Christmas be divided?) will be resolved peacefully. You hit send and then you wait.

You have no idea what the response will be. You have no idea if your child's other parent will agree to the items in your email or if you'll be blasted for

a) why you are an awful person

b) how you are an awful parent

c) both a and b.

Although you have done everything right in trying to communicate your child's needs/wants, you aren't communicating with a rational person. You aren't communicating with someone who is reading your email and understanding that you have your children's best interests at heart. You aren't communicating with someone who understands the lengths you have gone to try and reduce the conflict between you, not increase it. You aren't communicating with someone who can manage their emotions enough to understand that criticizing you as a person and a parent will not change you, it will only create further conflict.

You are communicating with someone who flips everything you say and do into a negative. You are communicating with someone who will always do the opposite of what you ask for, even if it hurts or disappoints the kids, simply because you asked for it. You are communicating with someone who doesn't have the ability to manage their behaviour enough to just answer your email with a simple yes or no. They have to give you a long explanation of why you are a horrible parent and/or person - and they may not even answer the question from the original email.

One of three things generally happen once you hit send;

1) The other parent emails you back within 15 minutes criticizing you for all your faults as a parent/person and refuses to allow whatever it is you have asked for in your email.

2) The other parent emails you back 24 - 72 hours criticizing you for all your faults as a person/parent and agrees to what you've asked for in your email.

3) You never get a response to your email. You're just left in limbo land.

If you are experiencing a high conflict separation or divorce, the above email communication pattern likely sounds familiar.

Parents experiencing high conflict separations and divorces often feel alone, isolated, confused and scared. Communication with someone who is irrational often results in becoming irrational yourself which can result in self-doubt, depression and a feeling of hopelessness.

Understanding the pattern of communication with a person who may have a high conflict personality will allow you to have less fear, anxiety and stress around communication with your child's other parent.

Unknowns are terrible - regardless of what they are. Removing the unknown from how your communication will unravel with a parent who may have a high conflict personality, will allow you to relax and feel less stress and anxiety during communications with your co-parent.

Three Communication Patterns of High Conflict Parents:

1) There will always be a negative statement about you as a person or you as a parent in their email communication with you. If the other parent is high conflict, they are incapable of not criticizing you. Expect it rather than be shocked by it. At the end of the day, they are just words. The words can only hurt you if you let them. Practice disengaging from the hurtful words and focus only on the content of the email that pertains to the children.

2) The emails you receive will be long winded, with little to no actual child related content, 95% of the time. Don't let your emotions get tricked into believing anything else is true. 95% of the content in the long winded email will be criticisms about you as a person and/or your parenting skills. Find a friend or professional who can read the emails for you and tell you if there is anything of importance in them. If there is nothing of importance related to the children – do not respond.

3) The perceptions of the other parent will be different from your perceptions. Arguing with the other parent over what either of you believes to be true will get you nowhere, except an ugly email exchange. Who cares if the other parent believes you fed the children hot dogs for breakfast, lunch and dinner while camping one weekend, even though they know you are a strict vegan and would never do that. It's not worth arguing about. Nothing you say/write will change their perception of what happened while you were camping, even though they weren't there and have no idea what really happened. Parents who are high conflict see the world through a different lens than those who aren't high conflict. In their reality, you really did feed the kids hot dogs for all of their meals even though you are a vegan and they can't help themselves but to comment, negatively, about your choices.

Understanding who you are parenting with, and what to expect from their email communications will allow you the freedom to disengage from the conflict, decide whether or not to respond, and deliver the appropriate message when you do.

# CHAPTER 10

# Do You Have
# Hamster Wheel Syndrome?

Is your conflict spiraling out of control? Do you feel like you are racing around in circles and getting nowhere? Does it seem like whatever fire you put out, another surfaces? Are you always on guard, waiting for the next crazy issue to arise? Does it feel like you're on a hamster wheel, racing to keep ahead of any potential conflicts, unable to jump off for a breather - for fear that if you relax (even for a minute) - you'll be side swiped by another accusation or manipulation? I call this the Hamster Wheel Syndrome.

When we keep doing the same things over and over but expecting different results. Attempting to micro-manage someone's potentially irrational behaviour in hopes of protecting both yourself and your children is exhausting by putting out any fires before they start. And let's be honest, micro-managing the potential fires isn't getting you anywhere, is it?

I'm guessing you are still shocked by the depth of control your co-parent still tries to have over you. You may be angry and frustrated by the subtle manipulations that are focused at hurting you (and therefore your children) - but no one else seems to see or understand them. You may be saddened by your inability to think or rationalize your way out of what seems like an impossible situation. You may be stunned at your co-parents inability to see how his/her behaviour is affecting your children, and I'm guessing that everyone once in a while, you are successful at putting a fire out. You let your shoulders relax a little. You take a few deep breaths, hoping that you can finally move forward with a sense of normalcy and peace. And then out of nowhere, wham! A nasty accusation via email, three pages long. You're served with a 79 page affidavit and court application for sole custody, both filled with lies. Your kids tell you that they just got back from a trip to Victoria, that you knew nothing about, and you have a Court Order that stipulates each parent requires approval to travel outside of Calgary.

Your co-parent just signed up to coach little league (which on the surface sounds awesome - what an involved parent), only you know it's so that they can monitor when the kids show up to practice or not, then criticize you for it later. So, you are back on to the hamster wheel, thinking that if you could just stay two steps ahead of the irrational behaviour, you'll be ok. Your kids will be ok. Except that there is no way to stay two steps ahead, to effectively micro-manage, irrational behaviour, or those few fires you were successful at putting out before they happened. I'm guessing they aren't the norm.

I know how hard you worked to stay two steps ahead, to catch the fires before they burned out of control. I also know how exhausting it is to try and stay on the hamster wheel, indefinitely, to continuously try to out-think irrational thinking.

Slowly, you start to think that maybe you've gone a little crazy yourself. That maybe you are the problem. That if you could just be a better person, better parent, you wouldn't have so much conflict with your co-parent. Slowly, the stress your body feels having been on a never ending hamster wheel starts to take its toll. You are sleeping less, catching more colds and picking fights with friends. You have less patience with your children, you are forgetting important meetings and your level of depression and/or anxiety is increasing. How do you stop? How do you surrender to your inability to micro-manage a conflict that hasn't arisen yet? How do you re-learn how to relax, when each time you've tried, you have been hit with another 'wham'. How do you jump off the Hamster Wheel? You do it one minute at a time.

Let me explain:

The fire is not the problem. As soon as you put out one fire, another one will take its place. That, I can guarantee you. The fire or the issue is not the problem, once one fire or issue is resolved, another fire or issue will always surface.

If you are co-parenting with someone who may have a high conflict personality, new fires or issues will continually pop up. People who may have a high conflict personality do not have the skill set to manage their emotions nor moderate their behaviour, so for them, fires/issues are a way to stay connected, because they cannot manage their emotions nor moderate their behaviour, they will just keep creating fires. Over and over and over...

So, instead of continuing to suffer from Hamster Wheel Syndrome, trying to micro-manage the next potential conflict that you know will happen, you just don't know when – jump off the wheel and choose to disengage from any potential conflict that might/will end up on your door step. Trust yourself to decide how best to handle the conflict once it arises and create some firm boundaries so you have the time and space necessary to deliver your response to the conflict appropriately.

## Disengage

You are strong enough to cope with whatever conflict arises, regardless of how ill prepared you were for its arrival. You are not defined by the negative words being shot at you. Only you can jump off the hamster wheel, no one else can do it for you.

## Decide

Is the conflict real or imagined - not all conflict needs to be responded to. You have a choices when presented with a conflict with regards to how you wish to proceed. You have time to reflect on your choices before giving a response, decisions do not need to be made immediately, although your high conflict co-parent will have you believe a decision is needed ASAP - that's just their opinion/perception - it doesn't have to become yours.

You can ask for help. When presented with a conflict and you don't know how to proceed, ask for help from someone who is not emotionally attached to the outcome. Sometimes a fresh set of ears/eyes is exactly what a conflict needs in order to be resolved effectively.

## Deliver

How you deliver your response to the conflict presented is key. Are you communicating your response the way you would want to hear it? Or the way your co-parent would want to hear it? Know your audience. Are you adding to the conflict through your choices in words? Tone?

Is your response Brief, Informative, Friendly and Firm?

To learn effective strategies to help you Disengage from your conflict, Decide how best to proceed and Deliver an appropriate response to your conflict.

# CHAPTER 11

# The #1 Reason
# You Get Triggered

It happens to the best of us. You go about our days/weeks/months actively disengaging from the conflict your co-parent likes to send your way, and it's working. Your hard work practicing disengagement is paying off.

You're sleeping at night (or at least some nights), you're obsessing about how to fix the conflict less and you're starting to laugh and relax a little. And you think you've nailed it... that you've succeeded in not letting your co-parent trigger you. You catch a glimpse of what freedom looks like. Freedom from over analyzing. Freedom from being controlled. Freedom from the little voice in your head that took so much work and effort to quiet. Freedom from the agonizing roller coaster of emotions you used to let flood over you whenever your co-parent would strike. And that freedom feels good. It feels normal. You start to feel normal, like you have the tools and strategies to cope with whatever might get sent your way. Feeling normal builds confidence, and when you're feeling confident, you're better able to manage your emotions so that you can utilize flexible thinking and moderate your behaviour. No more 3am middle of the night wake ups feeling the need to defend yourself from the attacks you read in an email the day before, and then it happens out of nowhere, like a slap in the face or a punch to the gut.

Your co-parent blindsides you with something you thought you would be prepared to handle. You rage with anger. Or cry in frustration. Freeze in fear. Your blood turns to ice. You can't breathe. Your brain shuts off. Your resolve to disengage doesn't just crumble - it shatters into a million pieces.

You bounce back and forth between disappointments in yourself, and you may question yourself, "How could I be so stupid? I never should have let my guard down." You have nothing but sheer hatred for your co-parent's actions/words/manipulations. You are 100% stuck in an emotion, or multiple emotions. It may very well be the worst feeling(s) you've ever felt. "I can't do this anymore." "I want to just give up." "I'm calling my lawyer and we're going to court."

"How much does a hit-man cost?" (We've all thought it - we just don't act on it!) Do not act on it. You will end up back in the dark hole.

The dark hole feels like waves of anxiety sporadically washing over you; or tirelessly running on the hamster wheel; micro managing in an attempt to stay in control of something (anything!); shutting down and not functioning; eating yourself out of house and home. You've been triggered. When it happens, you think all these new feelings (that are actually old feelings) are here to stay. Forever. That your dark hole is going to become your new norm. You forget that you have skills. That you've been in the dark hole before and crawled out. That you can move your emotions and become sane again. No one is sane while stuck in emotions.

When you're triggered, the feelings you feel are intense, all-consuming and terrifying. When you're triggered, you fall back into old patterns. Unhealthy patterns. Triggers are tricky little buggers. Popping up out of nowhere when you least expect them. Testing you to see if they can poke at your weak spots, which is what makes triggers interesting.

You may think your triggers are caused by your co-parent's actions/words/manipulations that trigger you. What if I told you your triggers were caused by you? That you were triggered because of something you "did", "said", "felt."

Your triggers are different than my triggers. We both have a high conflict personality in our lives; yet what triggers you is different from what triggers me. It's not because the high conflict personality in your life is any worse than the one in my life. And it's not because you have 'more on your plate to manage so it's harder for you, and it's certainly not because I'm smarter and have more skills than you.

I spent two weeks a few months ago hanging out in a triggered state. I ate all the food in the house and I started gravitating towards sweat pants. I was snapping at those around me and I wasn't sleeping. It took me 2 weeks of hanging out in the dark hole before I made any effort to get out. I had to force myself off my self-induced hyper attentive state to figure out what had happened.

Even those with tons of skills and practice managing triggers, get triggered. What triggers you, likely wouldn't trigger me. Just like what triggers me, likely wouldn't trigger you. What triggered me to eat for two weeks straight, snap at my loved ones and lose sleep would likely make you roll your eyes, but that trigger put me into a two week tailspin. And that trigger had nothing to do with what the high conflict personality person in my life said or did. It was 100%

on me. I went into self-doubt mode; criticizing myself for not seeing the trigger coming; for not managing it better; for not staying on the hamster wheel so I could have foreseen the future and avoided the trigger altogether. Thankfully, years of practice has taught me that hanging out in the dark hole doesn't have to last long. Don't get me wrong, two weeks of hanging out in a dark hole feels like an eternity.

A lot of long walks later, I was able to let go of the emotion around what triggered me and figure out why I had let myself get triggered. I got too busy. The #1 Reason you get triggered is you get too busy. It is as simple as that. When you get busy, you get lazy. And when you get busy (and lazy), you don't practice all the strategies you have implemented to manage your triggers. All those skills that allow you to sleep better, relax more, enjoy life again.

There is no reason to self loathe when you get triggered, no reason to hang out in the dark hole for too long. The #1 thing you can do to help yourself manage your triggers is to stop being too busy to practice your disengagement skills. You don't get triggered because your co-parent is a lying and manipulative crazy person.

You don't get triggered because you let your guard down; started to relax and laugh more. You don't get triggered because you got off the hamster wheel. You get triggered because you get too busy.

Take time to evaluate where you are at the end of the each day. Listen to your voice when it says you're doing/thinking/being too much; that busy-ness has taken over, and then stop. Use that opportunity to engage with yourself and slow down, so that when that next trigger appears, you'll be able to move right through it.

# CHAPTER 12

# OMG!
# Am I High Conflict?

Every parent I speak with asks me the same question, "What if I am the one who is high conflict?" My answer is always the same, "If you are the parent who is high conflict, you wouldn't be asking me if you were the high conflict parent."

The High Conflict Institute defines a high conflict parent as someone who lacks the ability to have insight into their own behavior, who doesn't have the ability to reflect on their actions and who blames others for everything that has gone wrong.

So if you're asking me if you are the high conflict parent, the answer is "No" because the high conflict parent wouldn't have the insight or self-reflection to question their own behavior and ask the question in the first place.

Now, that's not to say that your actions aren't contributing to the conflict.

Here are three ways you may be contributing to the conflict:

## 1. Do you react to the attacks against you and your ability to parent.

People who may suffer from a high conflict personality (HCP) thrive on drama. The more you react, the more empowered they feel to continue with their attacks. HCP's love to criticize and find fault in everything you say and do. Recognize this for what it is and don't emotionally attach yourself to their words or defending yourself.

It doesn't matter what you say to defend yourself, you will never change your HCP co-parent's opinion of you, so stop trying. When the nasty, manipulating, condescending emails pop into your inbox, prepare yourself for their ridiculousness before you read them.

Ask yourself how much crazier and critical can he/she be of me, and I promise you, each email will be just a little bit worse than the last one. So if you know it's going to be awful, you know his or her opinion of you is going to get worse, and you know nothing you can say will change it – why do you keep reacting? If you haven't disengaged from your co-parent sufficiently to be able to disregard the attacks, don't read the emails. Have a friend, family member or professional edit out the attacks for you so that the only portion of the email you see are the child related topics.

Every time you react to the attacks, you are fueling the HCP's fire to continue with even more attacks.

Stop reacting.

## 2. Do your words mimic your actions?

Parents in conflict tend to get triggered when attacked. Then they react to the attacks. And then they calm down and respond to the attacks/child related information. What often ends up happening is that their reaction is different from their response, which sends a mixed message to their co-parent.

While a simple apology for the mixed message may work with someone who doesn't have HCP, if your co-parent has HCP tendencies, any mixed messages you send will only further fuel their drama cycle. If you say no to changing the schedule, then a week later agree to change the schedule – you are telling your co-parent that they can continue to attack and manipulate you to get what they want, and that is definitely not the message you want to be sending. Be deliberate in your responses.

Take 48 hours to disengage from any digs or attacks, to process the request and how it may affect your day-to-day living, to decide whether or not the request works for the kids. Ensure that when you do respond, you do so with a well thought out answer that will not change.

## 3. Do you over-share information?

I'm guilty of this. It often feels like I have 12,000 thoughts racing through my head during any given second, and I like to share them all. Because sharing what I'm thinking helps me figure out what it is I'm actually feeling or thinking or wanting or needing. It's important to understand how you are actually feeling or thinking or wanting or needing.

I told you in Rule #2 to be deliberate about how you respond. How can you be deliberate if you aren't sure what it is you are actually feeling/thinking/wanting/needing? If you are one of those people who process information through sharing, that isn't going to change just because your co-parent might be an HCP. If you stop over-sharing in an attempt to be deliberate, you'll end up self-imploding. Trust me, I've tried it. It wasn't pretty. Over-sharers are verbal processers. They figure out their stuff by talking. And once they are done talking, they'll forget half of what they said and remember only their 'aha', that's what I'm actually thinking/feeling/wanting/needing.'

There is nothing wrong with being an over-sharer, you just have to be careful who you over share with. Over sharing with an HCP co-parent is a recipe for disaster. The more you say, the more likely an emotion is going to be expressed – giving an HCP ammunition to use against you in the future. If you happen to be an over sharer, find a friend, family member or professional you can over share with to figure out your 'aha's and then be deliberate in the message you send.

## CHAPTER 13

# Crumbs In
# The Butter Conflict

The dinnertime rule in our home is as follows: Eat as much dinner as you want or don't want, but if you don't eat what is on your plate, there is nothing else until breakfast the next morning. The kids know this rule inside out and backwards. Sometimes they push back, angling for a snack without having finished dinner first, but always without success. This is a firm rule in our home, until I found myself arguing with my kids about how many carrots they had to eat at dinner before they could be excused - five or seven carrots. I'm sure you can figure out which I was in favor of.

"There are kids starving in Africa," flew out of my mouth. To which my son replied, "Then give them my carrots." It was an exhausting 45-minute experience. By the end, I was 100% out of patience. Arguing about carrots is tough work. Sure, I was attempting my deep breathing disengagement strategies, but behind the deep breathing was a seething, frustrated, self-proclaimed 'worst mother in the world' parent lamenting because 45 minutes had just been wasted arguing over carrots. Two carrots, to be exact.

I called my sister and relayed the evening's events to her, looking for empathy, someone to understand the anguish those horrific 45 minutes caused me. Her response? "Why did you engage?" I had a list of excuses: "They need to respect the food put in front of them." "They need to get enough veggies in their diet." "They didn't eat their apples at lunch." "There are kids starving in Africa." (Surely my sister could appreciate this fact more than my kids did). "They don't get enough exercise so they need to eat better." "I'm too busy to be dealing with picky/fussy eaters." "I just want to be able to enjoy dinner without fighting with the kids." "I spent 30 minutes getting dinner ready and no one ever says thank you." "I….." And suddenly I realized why I engaged in the 45-minute carrot argument. I was tired.

I was mad about something a colleague said to me earlier in the day. I was thinking about a paper I had to write. I was frustrated about something that happened at work. I was feeling embarrassed that I was feeding the kids carrot and boxed pasta and jarred spaghetti sauce with hotdogs for dinner. I picked a fight with my kids over two carrots because I wasn't present, I wasn't clear on my end goal, I was unhappy. Because I wasn't where I needed to be in my head, I let our long standing dinnertime rule disappear and I picked a fight with the kids over two carrots.

I ruined my mood, the kids' moods, the dog's mood and the game of monopoly we were going to play when dinner was over – all over two carrots. There was no danger in the kids not eating two carrots; they would not have starved to death.

I call these types of fights "Crumbs in the Butter Conflict."

Crumbs in the Butter Conflict Definition: An argument that your ego has attached itself to winning, but is not life threatening for anyone involved, regardless of who wins or loses the argument. Actual crumbs in the butter are one of my biggest pet peeves. I see those little black and brown flecks in the beautiful, creamy yellow butter and my blood instantly boils.

Unfortunately, for me, my spouse could care less about crumbs in the butter. Ditto for my kids and they make zero effort to try and keep the butter clean and crumb free. I used to get so angry at their inability to see the crumbs, to not even try to be aware of them so that they could pick them out, so that I wouldn't have to suffer through having to look at them. Again, it was my sister, who pointed out the obvious, "Why are you engaging?"

Because it drives me crazy! Because they are doing it to annoy me! Because they only care about themselves! Because they are being lazy! Because I don't ask for much, could they do this one thing for me?

Sister brilliance: "They aren't trying to drive you crazy, they just don't care, so they don't put in the effort. It's you who is making a big deal over this. Get your own butter that only you use and move on."

So I tried out her theory. I got my own butter. I didn't tell anyone about my secret butter stash. No one else seemed to care about the crumbs in the butter; surely they wouldn't care if I had my own crumb free butter, and a really neat thing happened. My spouse and children continued to leave crumbs in their butter, but I no longer got angry about it. And that's how Crumbs in the Butter Conflicts work.

They seem like a really good idea at the time, but after a little reflection (or when your sister calls you out) you realize the argument might be more about you than the actual topic you are arguing about. With a little creative thinking (or call to your sister) you can resolve the Crumbs in the Butter Conflict for yourself, so that you aren't affected by the conflict anymore.

What Crumbs in the Butter Conflicts are you engaged in? Are you arguing over who will volunteer for little Suzie's field trip? Have you ever found yourself in an argument about what kind of toothpaste you use in your home versus the kind used in your co-parents home? Or how about an argument over what 'Suzie' eats for lunch (or doesn't eat for lunch.) Or an over argument over gloves versus mittens? Soccer versus baseball? Short hair versus long hair? 7:30pm bedtime versus 7:45pm bedtime? These are all Crumbs in the Butter Conflicts.

Remember: Crumbs in the Butter Conflicts are not life threatening. No one is going to get hurt if bedtime is a little later than usual. Little Suzie might be grumpy the next day, but she isn't going to be hurt. Soccer versus Baseball? Both are sports, both get Suzie active. Does it matter which one she plays? The next time you find yourself in an argument with your co-parent, ask yourself if it's a Crumbs in the Butter Conflict.

Five Questions to ask yourself whether or not your conflict is a Crumbs in the Butter Conflict:

1.  Will anyone die or get hurt if I disengage from this conflict/argument?

2. Am I worried that losing this argument will set a precedent?

3. Why am I trying so hard to win this argument?

4. What are 3 possible alternative outcomes to this argument?

5. In 10 years' time, will the outcome of this conflict be of any value?

# CHAPTER 14

# Four Kick-Ass Strategies To Give You Hope During Your High Conflict Separation Or Divorce

You want nothing more than to have the 'white picket fence' divorce. You know the kind; where you and your children's other parent can attend parent teacher interviews together, celebrate birthdays with one birthday party, sit beside each other at Christmas Pageant's and have coffee to figure out what the summer holiday schedule will look like.

You want your children to have a 'regular childhood' even though their parents are divorced.

You want your co-parent to be happy, to find someone else to share their life with who makes them happy, to move on with their lives. So you keep trying.

You tell yourself that your kids need you to keep trying. If you stopped trying, what message would that send to them? You keep searching Google for "strategies" or "possibilities." For anything that might give you a glimmer of hope that there is a better way.

I call this the Cycle of Hope:

- ✓ Stress builds in the high conflict parent– there is a breakdown of communication, the optimist parent becomes anxious and feels the need to placate their co-parent (unintentionally).

- ✓ Explosion – the high conflict parent explodes with verbal and emotional attacks – anger, blaming, arguing, threats, intimidation and manipulations. There must be a better way – The optimist says themselves "That will never happen again, I will find a better way to do this" and the Google search begins.

- ✓ Hope – Somewhat amicable communication between parents, the optimist feels a glimmer of hope that maybe 'this time the strategy worked' and the cycle will end.

## Repeat

The Cycle of Abuse and the Cycle of Hope are similar – for sure, but the similarity I want you to focus on is this – both include a high conflict person who will not change. No amount of Google searches will give you strategies to change the other person, your co-parent. They will not change. They do not have the insight or ability to manage themselves sufficiently to implement the strategies they need to implement in order to change, and because you are living the Cycle of Hope, you keep hoping and researching possibilities and strategies to try that will change the dynamic between you and your co-parent.

You are not a victim. You have hope, you are an optimist, and your optimism has finally paid off. The Cycle of Hope has paid off, only you don't need to be on the Cycle of Hope anymore, you can jump off and hang out in your life.

Below are 4 kick-ass strategies that will allow you to continue being an optimist, to give you hope, while stopping the Cycle of Hope:

- ✓ Your co-parent is NOT going to change. Stop hoping they will. Nothing you say or do will get them to change. Nothing. Stop defending yourself against their attacks; it will only encourage them to attack more.

- ✓ Disengage from the conflict – this takes time, do the work – you won't regret it. If your co-parents attacks are still triggering you, you are still engaged. Love and Hate are on the same spectrum. Your goal is to get to a place of indifference.

✓ Decide what is worth your time and what isn't. Write down five important child related topics you feel strongly about – that are worth your time and energy engaging in communication with your high conflict co-parent about. Having a plan about what you will and won't engage in conversation about gives you the freedom to opportunity to decide not to respond to the daily attacks and manipulations.

✓ Deliver the message you want heard. Dr. Phil says, "If you always do what you've always done, you'll always get what you've always got." How you are communicating with your high conflict co-parent isn't working for you, you aren't getting the results you are hoping for. So change it.

You are not a victim. You have hope, you are an optimist. An optimist who now has the right tools and strategies needed to have confidence in your optimism, your hope for a better co-parenting relationship.

# CHAPTER 15

# High Conflict Divorce: The Cycle of Hope

Hope is one of my favorite words. It implies that regardless of how ugly and messy things are right now, in this moment... you believe there is a possibility that things might improve.

People who have hope are optimists. Optimists don't just take the crappy hand they were dealt and cope with it; they actively seek out options and possibilities to change the game. Without hope, you become a victim of circumstance; someone who chooses to live with the crappy hand they were dealt, rather than explore options to re-deal the cards. Without a doubt, if you are co-parenting with a high conflict person, your current circumstances are the worst of the worst. You are co-parenting with a manipulative, controlling, threatening and intimidating human being. You are constantly on guard, waiting for the next shoe to drop. Your character and your ability to parent are attacked on a regular basis. You can't say or do anything right, everything is twisted and manipulated into a negative.

If you have hope, you are not a victim, you are an optimist. Your mind doesn't hang out in 'poor me'. Your mind is constantly thinking, 'how can I make this better?' No one wants (or deserves) to be manipulated or controlled. No one wants to be abused or victimized. The word victim feels like shame, guilt, embarrassment, isolation, stupid, pathetic and "Oh my gawd, how did I let this happen to me?" A Google search of the word victim came up with this definition that stuck out for me: 'a person who is cheated or fooled by someone else, repeatedly.' In other words, a victim is a cuck-hold. It's not like you already didn't feel bad enough, but now it seems that you're also that person everyone is talking about, and that's not you. You are not a victim. You have hope. You are an optimist.

You are co-parenting with someone who is hell-bent on destroying you, who twists everything you say into a negative, and who manipulates words and situations to make you look bad. Yet you keep trying to find ways to improve the co-parenting relationship. Your mind is always looking for possibilities to make the co-parenting relationship better.

You think things like: "What if I tried only communicating by email, maybe then he/she would choose words more carefully?" "What if I only enrolled the kids in activities during the times that I have them, that way we don't need to agree on which activities to put the kids into?" "What if I made all the exchanges happen at school or daycare, then we wouldn't need to see each other?" "What if I just gave him/her everything they want, maybe then the attacks would end?"

A Google search of the word optimist said this: 'Optimist: a person who has an inclination to put the most favorable construction upon actions and events or to anticipate the best possible outcome.' Simply put, someone who continuously tries to figure out a solution to a problem, regardless of how challenging the problem may be. That sounds like more like you. You are relentless in your pursuit to find a 'better way.' You continually search for the latest proven techniques to help your high-conflict situation. You seek out the help of psychologists, lawyers, friends, family, psychics, Himalayan gurus – everyone and anyone who might provide you with a glimmer of hope that there might be a way to make the manipulations, control, fear, anxiety, shame and stress, stop. You are not a victim. You are an optimist. You are in the Cycle of Hope.

# CHAPTER 16

# Stop Being Nice:
# Five Things I Learned From
# The High Conflict Person In My Life

When we're little, we're taught to be nice, "Be nice to your teachers; Be nice to the doctor; Be nice to your friends; Be nice to your neighbors." But what does being nice really mean? Obviously, everyone will have a different definition for being nice. But the general definition would be similar.

Being Nice: Use your manners, don't ruffle any feathers, smile, don't complain, help others – or put others needs before your own. I was a rock-star at being nice – if there was an award to be won for being nice, I would have won it. I said all the right things at parties, acted the part I was expected to play, smiled at the right times, avoided conflict, put others needs ahead of my own.

People looking in on my life from the outside would have said I had a pretty charmed life: beautiful family, successful career, and a loving husband, "Andrea is so nice!" Which is what I think got me into the mess I was in. Being nice also made me a target. High Conflict People target nice people.

By nature, nice people are nice to the core. It's our natural instinct to be kind, to give 100% of ourselves to care for others. And when we find someone who acts nice, we're attracted to them. Nice people attract nice people – the Law of Attraction says so. Unknowingly, nice people also attract High Conflict People.

I define a High Conflict Person as someone who likely has an undiagnosed personality disorder – they aren't just conflictual – they are out of this world conflictual. They blame others for everything, lack insight into their own behavior, twist words to support their perceptions, charm and manipulate themselves into nice people's lives and then turn on them – slowly (and sometimes quickly) doing everything in their power to destroy the nice person. But how does this happen? How does a nice person, someone who is genuinely kind, loving and supportive end up in a relationship with someone who manipulates, lies, cheats and controls?

I'll tell you firsthand how it happened to me. "Andrea is so nice" also meant that "Andrea is so passive." I nicely and passively gave my heart to someone who I thought shared similar values and goals. Looking back, I realize that there were warning bells. But when you're nice and you think you've finally met someone who is just as nice as you are, you become deaf to the warning bells.

Make no mistake, I'm not a dummy. I'm trained in high conflict separation and divorce mediation – I knew what the warning bells would be, what to be alerted to, how to protect myself against ever becoming involved with a High Conflict Person – and I nicely and passively ignored them. Not for a second did I think I could be manipulated and charmed into entering a relationship with a High Conflict Person. That only happened to other people, not me, not with my skills. And then, 18 months into the relationship, crying on the kitchen floor, I realized I'd made the biggest mistake of my life. I was in a relationship with a High Conflict Person, and I thought I was screwed. I thought I was screwed because I knew you didn't just walk away from a High Conflict Person. High Conflict People either hold you on a pedestal or they are hell bent on destroying you, and all that went through my mind was that I was never going to be nice to anyone ever again, that being nice had gotten me into the mess I was in and I was never going to let myself be vulnerable like that.

I went to a counselor to try and process how I'd been so blinded – how could I be so dumb. It was the counselor who told me being nice was the same as being passive. I'd never made that connection before, but it made sense. By being nice I was putting others needs before my own – which meant I wasn't really living my life, I was living the life others thought I should be living. By not ruffling feathers, smiling instead of screaming – I was being passive in my life, in my choices – ensuring I was being nice – so that other people would feel comfortable. Fast-forward 10 years and this is what I've learned:

## Stop Blaming Yourself

Everyone and anyone is fair game to a High Conflict Person – if you've been conned or manipulated into a relationship with one – don't blame yourself. You were being nice and someone really charming and controlling took advantage of your niceness. High Conflict People are so skilled, so talented, so over the top awesome at their game that you didn't have a hope in hell of protecting yourself from their charm.

Be Kind, Not Nice

Being nice is the same as being passive. Instead, choose kindness. Kindness comes from a place of self-love – choosing to be kind because the gesture resonates with your character and your value systems rather than being nice because it's what you "should" be.

Being in a relationship with a High Conflict Person does not mean you're screwed, but it does mean you need to create firm boundaries to protect yourself, consistent communication strategies and a clear understanding of the importance of not reacting to the manipulations and threats that will continuously be thrown at you.

There is a light at the end of the tunnel. I had to dig deep, do a lot of learning, researching, reflecting and purposeful planning – but it paid off. If you are ready to commit to changing the dynamic between you and the High Conflict Person in your life – really ready – then there are strategies you can implement today to help you take back control of your life.

What didn't kill me, did make me stronger – it's a cliché – but one I live by. Without a doubt, learning how to disengage from the drama, implement boundaries and follow through on them, even when I really wanted to crumble, was the hardest and most challenging experience of my life. But also the most liberating. I have a skill set second to none – I have the ability to empathize and strategize during a crisis; I know how to communicate with High Conflict People and get results; I know that being nice is not a trait I want my kids to learn, instead I want them to understand the value of kindness.

You can survive your relationship with the High Conflict Person in your life, but you need to stop being nice, and start taking action to stop the manipulations and create a different dance moving forward.

# CHAPTER 17

# I Was Triggered – And Survived
## (Even Though My Pants No Longer Fit)

Because sometimes I like to eat my feelings rather than feel them, I had a 24-hour binge fest on foods I don't normally eat, which led to irrational thinking, poor decision-making and pants that didn't do up. What caused my lapse into the horrible place I like to call 'Planet Triggerdom?' Triggerdom is the world that only exists when you've been triggered – because when you've been triggered, you aren't sane or rational and it's as if you are living on a different planet: Planet Triggerdom.

## Judgment

I have pretty good boundaries in place to ensure I'm not easily triggered into Planet Triggerdom by the high conflict person in my life. I've worked long and hard to figure out exactly what I need to do and say so I don't get triggered into that insane place. But then I was judged by someone I wasn't expecting to be judged by and wham, it hit me like a slap in the face.

I wasn't being judged for something trivial like what outfit I was wearing, or what I chose to feed my kids. I wasn't even being judged by what kind of parent I was (My kids were a mess. Was there a full moon?) I was judged for a blog post I wrote. A blog post that revealed a little more of me than I usually like to share. I allowed myself to be vulnerable and someone judged me and it crushed me.

I was filled with self-doubt, angered by their lack of support, scared that they might be right – maybe I did reveal too much? And I spiraled into horrible, insane place called Planet Triggerdom.

Someone judged me and I felt defensive, I wanted to lash back at them, defend my actions, defend my story, and defend my need to be kind to myself even if it meant not being nice to others. Being nice is making other's feel good, even if it's at your own expense. Thank heavens I've had some experience in Planet Triggerdom.

Even though I was choosing to eat my feelings, my thinking was cloudy and I was spiraling into a defensive angry and anxious vortex – there was some tiny piece of me that had the wherewithal not to react with a nasty defensive email. 24 hours later, while shaking off a food coma, I had clarity on the judgment I had received.

Something I wrote made the person who judged me feel threatened. Their judging me had nothing to do with me and everything to do with them. It's almost impossible to remember that powerful little fact when we're in Planet Triggerdom – so write it down somewhere so you can see it, regularly.

*"Judgment has nothing to do with you and everything to do with the person making the judgment."*

So ignore them.

I had changed the steps to the dance that a reader was used to dancing with me, she wanted me to dance my old dance, so she did what she could to get back the familiar Andrea.

*"Judgment is about keeping people inside the safe bubble they've become familiar with."*

Pop the bubble.

I chose to eat myself out of house and home; I chose my spiral into Planet Triggerdom. I was triggered, and chose my reaction. I wasn't expecting judgment from the source that it come from, so my boundaries hadn't protected me from their words and criticisms. But at the end of the day, their words and criticisms only hurt me because I let them.

> *"Judgment, regardless of the source,*
> *only triggers us if we let it."*

Don't let it.

Judgment forces us into a really dark area of our brains. It makes us question ourselves, our choices and our decisions. Judgment pushes us into Planet Triggerdom when we least expect it. And Planet Triggerdom is an insane and lonely place. Judgment and Planet Triggerdom happens to everyone, even those with refined boundaries and conflict protection skills – so don't beat yourself up when it happens to you. Roll with Planet Triggerdom for 24-hours. Eat what you need to eat, spiral as far as you need to spiral – just don't react. Reacting will only trigger more judgment and trigger you further into Planet Triggerdom – and the further you go, the harder it is to get out.

> *"Judgment makes us mean to ourselves in our heads, but*
> *that only pushes us further into Planet Triggerdom.*
> *Be nicer to yourself in your head and your spiral into*
> *Planet Triggerdom won't last as long."*

Being judged sucks. Delving into Planet Triggerdom sucks worse. Learn to trust yourself, your skills and your coping mechanisms to know that the feeling will pass. And when the feeling passes, you will thank yourself for not reacting.

CHAPTER 18

# Five Strategies For Co-Parenting With A Narcissist For People Who Want To Stay Sane

Co-parenting with a Narcissist will make you feel like pulling your hair out, hourly. Perhaps you don't even know you are co-parenting with one? You just feel like you are spiraling out of control, stuck in a miserable vortex and unsure if you'll ever find your way out.

Below are some usual suspect phrases a narcissist co-parent may use:

✓ You must change the parenting schedule when they request it but it is never reciprocated.

✓ You must change the children's diet to reflect the newest fad diet your co-parent has read about (usually worded in such a fashion that presumes the food you feed the children is so nutritionally deficient it is causing them harm).

✓ You must dress the children in shorts and a t-shirt. It's too hot outside for them to be wearing jackets, they'll overheat and get dehydrated and it will be all your fault. And when it rains, you are scolded for not ensuring a rain jacket and rain boots were packed.

Do you notice the common theme, "You must?" Narcissist co-parents can't help themselves. They believe they are superior to you, that they have to tell you what to do or you won't know how to do it. But what's even more frustrating than constantly being told what to do is if you actually do as they tell you, and they still find fault in your actions.

If you are co-parenting with a narcissist, you can do no right. Starting to sound a little familiar?

**The DSM-IV defined Narcissistic Personality disorder as follows:** A pervasive pattern of grandiosity (in fantasy or behavior), need for admiration, and lack of empathy, beginning by early adulthood and present in a variety of contexts, as indicated by five (or more) of the following:

1) Has a grandiose sense of self-importance (e.g., exaggerates achievements and talents, expects to be recognized as superior without commensurate achievements).

2) Is preoccupied with fantasies of unlimited success, power, brilliance, beauty, or ideal love.

3) Believes that he or she is "special" and unique and can only be understood by, or should associate with, other special or high-status people or institutions.

4) Requires excessive admiration.

5) Has a sense of entitlement, i.e., unreasonable expectations of especially favorable treatment or automatic compliance with his or her expectations.

6) Is interpersonally exploitative, i.e., takes advantage of others to achieve his or her own ends.

7) Lacks empathy: is unwilling to recognize or identify with the feelings and needs of others.

8) Is often envious of others or believes others are envious of him or her.

9) Shows arrogant, haughty behaviors or attitudes.

## How do those traits play out in a co-parent?

✓ They are always right, you are always wrong.

✓ Zero insight into how their behavior affects the children.

✓ Extreme emotions – a flare for drama.

✓ Rigid thinking, only one solution to a problem – theirs.

✓ Manipulates language to suit their needs/ perceptions.

Do you see some narcissistic tendencies in your co-parent? Does it shed some light on the challenges you've been having trying to raise children with this person? If you are (or suspect you are) co-parenting with a narcissist, you need strategies that work to keep your sanity intact.

Your narcissistic co-parent is not intentionally trying to make you insane. But because they have no insight into their behavior, they don't realize they are making you crazy, they honestly believe they are helping you become a better person.

The five strategies for co-parenting with a narcissist are:

## 1) Disengage, Disengage, Disengage

Do whatever you need to do to emotionally disengage from the attacks, lies and manipulations your narcissistic co-parent repeatedly throws your way. They will not change. You know what they say to you isn't true, so stop letting it hurt you.

## 2) Understand your Triggers

You can't disengage if you are continuously being triggered. Make a list of 10 things your narcissistic co-parent says/does that trigger you. Being aware that you have been triggered is the first step in understanding your triggers. Every person has different triggers; what bugs you, may not bug me.

## 3) Create a Communication Plan

Your narcissistic co-parent will try and get you to dance the dance they want you to dance – but you need to hold firm on the communication plan you created for yourself. You are creating it for a purpose: to help you stay sane. Your communication plan will be created around your triggers. If face to face communication triggers you, only communicate by text and email. If you are constantly receiving condescending text messages, block the number and communicate only by email. You get the idea. The key is to create a plan to help you avoid triggers and implement it.

## 4) Stop Attack/Defend Behavior

**It** feels impossible not to respond to someone who has criticized your parenting, lied about your family and manipulated your words against you – but what good is responding? If you defend yourself, it just opens the door for your narcissistic co-parent to continue issuing insults. There is nothing you can say or do that will change your narcissistic co-parent's mind about how they feel about you. Save your time, energy and brainpower for more important things – like playing with your children.

## 5) Dance

There is no better way to stay sane when co-parenting with a narcissist than to kick up your heels, shake your shoulders and dance. Dancing is the number one stress reliever for quickly changing a person's mood. Try it, shake your shoulders – are they stiff? Mine were when I first started; I looked and felt like a robot, but I didn't quit. I was alone in my house, who cared what I looked like.

Whether it's country, rock and roll, pop or Jazz – put on a song you love and have a dance party in your kitchen. Seems simple, right? Try it — it's tricky at first, but you'll get the hang of it, and your sanity will thank you.

# CHAPTER 19

# I'm Done!

# The 4D's of High Conflict Divorce

I'm done. I quit. I can't do this anymore. I give up. It's exhausting trying to raise children with someone who hates you.

You're done. Done fighting. Done placating. Done brainstorming ways to make it better. Done taking the high road. Divorce is hard at the best of times. But when you divorce someone who may have a high conflict personality, it's a whole new ball game of hell.

Daily emails that read like novels about how you are the world's worst parent; how you are destroying your children with your horrific controlling behaviors; sentence after sentence about how your children would be better off without you. You try to be amicable. You create a shared calendar to keep everyone in the loop about kid's activities. You try to have conversations around what activities your kids should partake in. You try to engage in joint parent teacher conferences, get extra tickets for Christmas concerts and avoid saying anything negative about your Ex in front of your kids.

You've read every book you can get your hands on to try and learn about how to divorce the right way. Surely someone out there knows something you don't know about how to make your situation better. This can't be it – what is your life is going to look like for the next 18 years, living in constant fear of the next verbal attack, never knowing when you might get served with the next court application, being bad mouthed to family, friends, colleagues and your children. And no one understands the private hell you are going through. Everyone has an opinion. It's easy to have an opinion when you're not emotionally attached or when it's not your own kids who have to suffer the possible consequences.

## "Take Him To Court"

But real court isn't what it looks like on TV. You want to believe that a Judge will hear your story because you're being honest. But a Judge doesn't know that. You both have convincing stories. Besides, the Judge doesn't understand your children, their temperaments, their needs. A Judge would just order a cookie cutter parenting plan and wish you good luck.

Managing a life filled with drama, inconsistencies, lies and manipulations will take its toll on you – and your children – but the 4 D's of High Conflict Divorce can help: Disengage, Decide, Deliver and Document. Your divorce isn't like your friends divorce, yours is different. Your friends Ex understands how to put the kids needs before his/her own and they are working cooperatively together. Your Ex is trying to destroy you. What worked for your friend will not work for you. So stop trying. Stop idealizing the possibility that one day you and your Ex will have family dinners or amicable Christmas mornings together. Your divorce is high conflict. You need strong and secure boundaries, clear and concise communication and you need to document your Ex's manipulative behaviors.

## Disengage

You are in conflict with your child's other parent because their words and actions negatively trigger and affect you and your children. Like most parents, you will do anything to protect your children form harm –

physical, verbal and emotional. If you take the time to sort through your triggers and plan a strategy for how to cope when triggered, you will be putting yourself (and your children) on a path for healthier conflict resolution.

## Decide

You've likely never had to make so many decisions in your whole life. What will the parenting schedule be? Why does all the research contradict itself? Do I have to ask to get the kids haircuts? Parents in low levels of conflict have the luxury of being able to figure out a lot of their answers through regular communication, but you are not experiencing low levels of conflict, you are stuck in the murky and smelly destructive home of high conflict decision making. How do you make decisions when the person you have to make them with says no to everything you put forward just because they hate you? How do you ensure you are not triggered when you are communicating with your high conflict ex?

## Have An Agenda

If you have an agenda, you'll be more apt to refocus on what needs to be decided rather than steering off course indefinitely.

When communicating use proposals. Offer a proposal for what you would like the outcome to be – the other parent will say no, because that's what they do – but rather than let it stop at the no and stall the process, ask them to make an alternative proposal and don't take no for an answer. They will struggle – they don't really know what they want, so they'll try and create some drama (stay disengaged). Refocus and keep pushing for an alternate proposal.

## Deliver

When you are communicating with your High Conflict Ex, keep all emotional words out of your email. If you use an emotional word, your Ex will attach themselves to the emotional word and ignore everything else you've written. Keep your emails to four sentences. If you are writing more than four sentences, you are either sneaking in an opinion (and you will be attacked) or an emotion (you will also be attacked).

All communication should be child focused, emotion and opinion free and four sentences.

## Document

In jot note form document the facts surrounding each manipulation/lie your Ex attempts to control you with. Do not add in any emotions to your notes – just the facts. Include dates, times and outcomes. High Conflict People are crafty and charismatic – often manipulating those in perceived positions of power – in order to ensure your voice is heard, you need to provide a detailed document outlining the pattern of behavior that is causing you (and your children) harm. Emotional words give way to the 'he said she said' argument, so you want to ensure you keep all emotions out of your documentation. Include facts only – and ideally facts with corroboration (emails, texts, Our Family Wizard).

The 4D's of High Conflict Divorce won't change your Ex's behaviors. Nothing will change their behaviors, ever. There will be days you still want to quit, to walk away, to escape the insanity permanently. But, if you put the 4 D's of High Conflict Divorce into practice, the high road won't be as lonely and you might just preserve a little bit of your sanity during this insane time.

# CHAPTER 20

# High Conflict Sanity Saver

# Stop Attack/Defend Behaviour!

I have often heard parents say, "I hate my former spouse, you'll never guess what he or she just did/said." Whenever I hear one parent say he or she hates the other parent, I know they need to work on disengaging. Love and hate are on the same continuum. Both take up significant space in our lives. Love occupies space in our hearts, and hate occupies space in our minds. By hating the other parent, you are giving them valuable space in your head. That space could be better used to create a new way of engaging your children, dream of a new goal that you wish to attain, or imagine yourself successfully overcoming a challenge. By removing the hate from your mind, you provide yourself with opportunities to spend more time enjoying your life and being happy with your children rather than engaging in conflict with the other parent.

Your goal is to feel indifferent towards the other parent, regardless of the mudslinging they send your way. Indifference equates to disengagement.

When you are attacked in an email (or in person), your gut reaction is usually to react by defending yourself.

Practice disengaging from the need to defend yourself, rather than reacting. Take 24 hours to disengage yourself from the attacks and respond only to topics pertaining to your children. Easier said than done, but an imperative step to regaining your sanity while parenting with someone you are in conflict with.

You cannot change the attacks that are sent your way. Nothing you say or do will ever change the other parent; not their behavior, not their actions and certainly not the words they choose to use. The only thing you can do is to change how you respond to the other parent's behavior.

You can choose to disengage from the attacks. You can choose to respond only about what is important (your children). You can choose to stop defending yourself. Just because the other parent says something about you or to you, it doesn't mean you have to believe it or prove it wrong.

It is a choice to disengage and ignore the hurtful digs, lies and manipulations. It is a choice to give yourself time to respond, rather than react. It is a choice to stop defending yourself against someone who isn't listening anyways. And it's a choice to start regaining your sanity.

# CHAPTER 21

# You Want Me to What?

# High Conflict Divorce Boundaries 101

When you ask someone what he or she wants or needs, they usually begin by telling you what they don't want, "I don't want my ex to speak poorly of me in front of our kids." "I don't want the kids dropped off 15 minutes late at every exchange." "I don't want to receive 15 emails or texts a day telling me everything I do wrong as a parent." "I don't want to destroy our children's childhood experience because we can't stop arguing." "I don't want to have our kids worried about where their mom and dad will sit on their wedding day." "I don't want to fight anymore."

Very few people can actually tell you want they do want. Even when pushed, they will tell you what they don't want. And when you focus all your energy and attention towards what you don't want, you end up attracting just that, everything you don't want.

Boundary setting and implementing requires you to first figure out what you do want/need, "I need to feel safe in my home knowing the other parenting isn't going to walk in unannounced." "I want our children to be well adjusted adults." "I need to create effective communication strategies to ensure our children's needs are always met." "I need to be less angry/anxious."

A client of mine was concerned that her children's father was continuing to walk into the marital home unannounced, even though they had been separated for over three years. The father felt that because he was contributing to the mortgage and utilities, he had every right to walk into 'his house.' It was imperative that she create (and implement) a boundary to ensure her wants/needs and safety were respected.

The "want/need" – to have the children's father call or knock before entering the house rather than walking in unannounced.

The "boundary" – a conversation with the children's father around the confusion it creates for the children when their dad walks into the house unannounced when the kids know their parents are separated. It's sending a mixed message.

The "implementation" – once the boundary conversation has taken place, you must ensure you follow it. You must follow the boundary you created. If you slip, even once, your boundary will be discredited by the other parent and not followed.

The "follow through" – if you put a boundary in place, are firm in its implementation, and it's still not being followed, you will need to create consequences for the boundaries not being followed by the other parent.

For example:

"The boundary" – a conversation with the children's father around the confusion it creates for the children when their dad walks into the house unannounced when the kids know their parents are separated. It's sending a mixed message.

Suppose the other parent continues to walk in unannounced.

The "consequence" – the children find it confusing that you continue to walk in the house unannounced even though I've requested you call or knock first. My next step will be to change the locks, should you continue to walk into the house unannounced.

If the other parent continues to walk in unannounced after the "consequence" conversation, you must follow through and change the locks.

Creating boundaries will do nothing to move your situation forward if you do not implement them completely. This is why it's vital that you fully understand your wants/needs. You will have greater power (willpower) to follow through on the boundaries you have created, if you are clear on why you created them in the first place.

# Conclusion

What I Know for Sure (to steal a saying from Oprah)

You can't change other's. You can try, but you will fail. You <u>can</u> change how you respond to other's - and changing how you respond will set you free.

You can't rationalize with someone who is irrational. You can try, but you'll go crazy. You <u>can</u> choose to disengage from the irrational and focus on remaining calm, clear and concise.

Kids are resilient to change, to different parenting styles - to life in two homes. Kids are not resilient to ongoing parental conflict. It only takes one to stop the conflict. Be the one.

Just because someone says it doesn't make it true. Know who you are and what you believe in, then ignore the rest.

The high road is a lonely place, so few choose to take it. If I'm honest, I didn't always take it - but I sure tried and was successful about 75% of the time. It takes courage, intention and a strong support system - choose the high road and when your kids are older, and have the ability to reflect on their childhood, they will thank you.

It took me over a decade to learn how to disengage form the high conflict person in my life - go easy on yourself. Disengaging takes time and effort. It seems like an impossible task, the attacks and manipulations are endless, but if you want your freedom bad enough - if you have truly had enough of the drama - you'll put in the effort.

*Disengage. Decide. Deliver.*

Take control of your high conflict separation or divorce - you're worth it.

Made in United States
North Haven, CT
12 July 2023